Tasty Trails of

TASTY TRAILS OF NORTHUMBRIA

by
Jill Harrison

Dedication
To
Rosie and Dan

Published by Casdec Ltd
22 Harraton Terrace
Birtley
Chester-le-Street
Co Durham
DH3 2QG

Tel: (0191) 4105556
Fax: (0191) 4100229

Written by Jill Harrison

First Published September 1994

ISBN 0 907595 91 X

CONTENTS

Author's Note

Heatherland and bent land
Black land and white
God brings me to Northumberland
The land of my delight.

Like a good Northumbrian broth this book is made from all sorts of local ingredients. The food traditions of this county are as rich and varied as the wonderful scenery explored in these trails.

Our eating habits tell us so much about the society we live in and it is fascinating to see how tastes change. Porpoise pudding for example, once a medieval delicacy, has fortunately fallen out of favour. There are, however, new and exciting traditions being created all the time and each trail offers the chance to experience these first hand.

To all those farmers, fishermen, hoteliers and shopkeepers who are bringing these traditions alive I would like to extend my thanks for their help and enthusiasm.

The National Park, as caring custodian of much of the regions outstanding landscapes and the people who live there also deserves thanks, as do the National Trust and English Heritage who have preserved so many of the buildings and places of interest mentioned in this book.

I am also indebted to Josie Cummings for his photographic skills, my aunt, Maureen Emmerson for the illustrations and my family for their patience and sense of humour.

The historical material was chosen for its relevance to food and, while as accurate as such accounts allow, is not intended as a comprehensive history of the area. My thanks to the Local Record Office, History Societies and Libraries for help and advice.

The maps, which are not to scale, should be used only as a rough guide. An OS Map is invaluable for further exploration.

Trail One
Border Bread and Honey

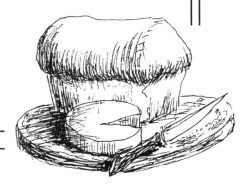

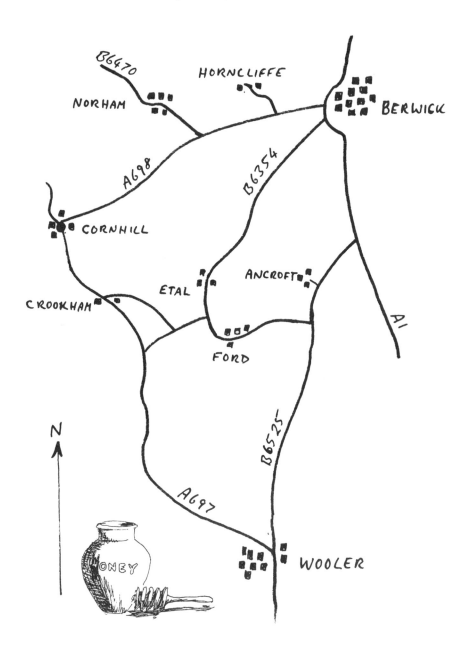

NOT TO SCALE

2

Border Bread & Honey

This trail which takes us along the borderlands of the Tweed, starts and ends in the historic town of Berwick.

Nestling at the mouth of this famous fishing river, Berwick is a fascinating town, revealing around every corner, secrets of its ancient and exciting history as a Border stronghold.

The name Berwick is thought to be derived from its situation, Aber meaning mouth and Wick, a town. More romantically it might refer to the bears which roamed in the nearby forests until the late middle ages. The town's coat of arms subscribes to this theory, depicting a ferocious bear amidst a tangle of trees.

Archaeological finds show that Berwick and the surrounding countryside had a rich culinary tradition. The hunters and fishers of the Bronze age, whose beakers and cooking pots are still being unearthed, enjoyed a rich and varied diet.

If you could catch them, there was a profusion of wild boar, beaver, roe deer and primitive wild cattle. Game birds such as capercailzie, grouse and black-cock were also abundant as were sheep and goats which had been introduced to the area as early as 4000 BC.

Variety was also the spice of Berwickshire life in the 1600's when a nobleman's larder might contain salmon, salt eels, sturgeon and an ornithologist's nightmare of mallard, teal, seagulls, curlews, quail, snipe, redshank, dotterils, buzzards, terns, larks and plovers. If it moved it was "fair game". A hen cost sixpence, a goose 1s 2d and swans, of which Berwick was full, 10 shillings.

Locally caught porpoise and seal were often sold to Newcastle fish market. In 1568 Lord Hudson, visiting Berwick wrote to Lord Cecil that sixty porpoises and "whorlpools" which were a large breed of dolphin had been killed and he had eaten "a part that night to supper".

Porpoise Pudding for the Nobility

Take the blood of him (*the porpoise I presume*) and the grease of himself and oatmeal and salt and pepper and ginger and mix these well together and then put this in the gut of the porpoise and then let it seeth easily and not hard, a good while, then take him up and broil him a little and then serve forth.

Local table manners were rather unrefined at this time, causing James IV when travelling in the area to say that he did not wish his food "touched with fingers, as that all men's fingers are not alike clean".

Before testing the infinitely more civilised modern eating establishments in the town a car park must be found. This can prove a very difficult task, but the large open square next to the Barracks is probably the best place to try and is also an ideal spot to start a walking tour. Presuming this is successful there are several places to explore in the immediate vicinity.

The church of The Holy Trinity of 1651, was the only church to be built during Cromwell's austere "Protectorship". Cromwell stayed briefly in Berwick during the Civil War, his troops looting and causing havoc. Despite its rather forbidding puritan exterior the church is blessed with a variety of beautiful stained glass windows and is well worth entering. No bell was allowed so the bell in the Guildhall just down the street is rung to announce the services.

The Barracks themselves offer an excellent insight into local life. It now houses a superb regimental museum for the King's Own Scottish Borderers and a museum and art gallery which includes part of the famous Burrell collection of artifacts.

The Barracks, which could accommodate thirty-six Officers, and six hundred men and their wives and children, were built in 1717 following bitter complaints by the townspeople that they were sick of billeting soldiers who constantly ate them out of house and home. This is hardly surprising as records show the huge amount of food they ate.

In 1586 a soldier in the garrison was allowed 24ozs of bread, a bottle of beer and 2lbs of beef or mutton each day. On the three "fish" days of the week he

4

could expect half pound of butter, 1 lb cheese, a quarter of a cod or a "reasonable piece of ling" and seven or eight white or red herrings. No meat was allowed during Lent, the penalty being several hours in the pillory or a night in the stocks. Civilians could be punished with four to six days imprisonment while a poor soldier might get twenty days on bread and water. The bread price varied in accordance with the harvest. In 1504 wheat cost 5s 8d a quarter and by 1521 it had risen to 20s thus causing great hardship.

After digesting all this history a cup of coffee is needed. Walking down Church Street, one can't miss The arcaded Town Hall which is now an interesting interesting Gift Shop and Coffee House. Here a homemade cheese scone and a piece of carrot cake will fortify the visitor for further exploration. This site has a long culinary history. In the middle ages the weekly markets were held here. When the Town Hall was built in 1750 in the style of London's St Martin in the Fields, complete with spire, the east ground floor was used to sell local meat, poultry and dairy produce. Berwick was famous for its veal which came from Haggerston.

Berwick High Street was also the scene of a thriving market which served the country for miles around. It was an exciting and sometimes dangerous place to visit. From 1300 two weekly and three annual markets attracted hundreds of shaggy black cattle and wild eyed horses with their expectant owners on the look out for a good time among the flesh pots of Berwick.

Berwick Market. 1890's

5

There was also a fish market, selling cockles and mussels from Budle Bay and Holy Island and an abundance of local white fish. A haddock measuring thirty two inches and weighing eleven and three quarter pounds was sold in the 1800's for 1s 6d.

Local gardeners took stalls to sell their surplus produce and there was always a supply of cabbages, potatoes, leeks, peas, carrots, radishes, artichokes, celery, lettuces and cucumbers. A local remarking that "These garden stuffs are all good of their kind and cheap".

At one time there were fifty nine pubs in the town, providing plenty of choice for the many visitors. Robert Burns came here but was sadly most unimpressed. Charles Dickens also came to give two readings of his works at the Assembly Rooms.

Good food has always been important to the people of Berwick. Directly across the road from the Town Hall is Fairbairns, the Butchers. As might be expected in a prime stockrearing area, the meat here is excellent, well hung and dressed. Their own meatloaf, potted meat, haggis and pressed tongue are equally good. They also make an unusual salt beef, Cumberland sausage with herbs and roast their own pork.

Almost next door is the "Food Shop", a well stocked delicatessen which sells Lindisfarne Mead, Chainbridge honey, Heatherslaw Mill cakes and biscuits and Redesdale Dairy sheep and goat cheese.

A speciality of the town in times past was Berwick May Day Tarts, baked to celebrate a much anticipated day of festivity when the Riding of the Bounds took place. These can no longer be bought but are well worth making and are not as complicated as the recipe might suggest.

Berwick May Day Tarts

5 ozs plain flour
1 oz lard
1 $^1/_2$ oz salted butter
2 ozs unsalted butter,
softened
2 oz caster sugar
1 beaten egg

1 oz ground almond
1 oz chopped peel
2 ozs currants
almond essence or
rose water to taste
lemon glace icing

Rub the lard and salted butter into the flour and mix to a stiff pastry dough with a little cold water. Roll out and line 12 2^1/2" well greased tartlet pans. Cream together the unsalted butter and sugar and beat in the egg. Sift in the almonds, add the peel, currants and flavouring and mix thoroughly. Fill the pastry shells. Use any scraps to make decorations on each tart. Bake at 400F for 7 mins, then reduce to 350F for a further 15 mins. While still warm trickle the lemon icing over them.

Despite Berwick's chequered history, one year Scottish, the next English, it has always had the fruits of its farming and fishing community to help the local economy. Salmon from the Tweed and the estuary at Berwick are still rightly world famous.

As early as 1764 Berwick's Old Shipping company carried passengers and salmon to London on their clipper ships in the greatest style and quickest time. Today the Berwick Salmon Fisheries PLC and Ralph Holmes and Son carry on this fishing and processing tradition.

R. Holmes. Fish, Game & Poultry Dealers. C. 1890

The Holmes family are unique in the business having been established in their Bridge Street premises since 1760. From here they retail and wholesale wild salmon, grilse and trout. Today it is run by a fifth generation, also Ralph and his mother Evelyn.

Berwick Salmon

To cook a salmon 'Berwick fashion', the fish has to be "crimped". This means that it is steaked, then each steak cut through the middle, so making it chop shaped. Bring a pan or fish kettle of well salted water to the boil. Cook at one minute to the pound of the original weight of the fish. Drain well and serve hot with melted butter, cucumber and new potatoes and peas. The cooking liquid which is called "Dover" from the Celtic d'ovor, can be reduced to make a thin sauce.

Mrs Holmes recalls the days when business was so good that the family kept a suite of rooms in one of London's best hotels as a base for its export trade continues built on their excellent reputation, but the stocks of salmon have dwindled due to disease and over fishing at sea.

The Holmes family net their fish at the special 'stations' all along the Tweed, which they have used for hundreds of years. Many of them are smoked in their original old smokehouse, ready for instant sale to hotels, tourists and the local population.

Salmon Fishers, Berwick-on-Tweed

Salmon Netting on the Tweed

In Dr Fullers wonderful history of Berwick, published in 1799, he tells how the ability to pack the salmon in ice enabled it to be sent all over the country. Before this the salmon had to be boiled and put into 'kits' or barrels to preserve it while it was transported.

Several ice houses were built in the town, filled with giant blocks of ice brought in the holds of ships from Russia and hauled up into the town with horse and cart. Dr Fuller wrote that they had to be built on an east or south east aspect for the advantage of the morning sun expelling the damp air. Ralph Holmes' ice house with its thick stone walls, which was only recently sold, faced north with no ill effects.

Lobsters were a sought after delicacy in Dr Fullers day and were sold in the market or carried from door to door in baskets. He remarked with admiration that the "circumstances of lobsters throwing off their shells once a year and reproducing them, as well as the reproduction of a claw when lost by accident, constitutes two phenomena in nature truly wonderful and not unworthy of the contemplation of the philosophic mind."

The herring kept the village of Spittal, on the south side of the estuary, in business for many years. At the turn of the century trade with Europe resulted in a thriving pickling, curing and smoking industry which employed large numbers of local girls and brought prosperity.

Herring Gutting at Spital

Stuffed Herring

4 herrings	*1 tbspn lemon juice*
1 tbspn chopped parsley	*1 oz soft white breadcrumbs*
1 tbspn chopped thyme	*seasoned flour*
1/2 tbspn grated lemon rind	*1 oz browned breadcrumbs*

Wash and dry herrings and clean them. Mix herbs, lemon juice and rind and white breadcrumbs. Stuff the fish with this then roll them lightly in well seasoned flour. Melt a little dripping in a baking pan and when very hot add herrings. Cook in the oven at 350F for twenty minutes. Sprinkle with the browned crumbs and return them to the oven for five minutes before serving.

Further along Bridge Street is Elizabeth Middlemiss's restaurant "Funny-waytemekaliving". The name is as imaginative and original as her cooking, which has won several prestigious awards and acclaim in the national press. Everything is homemade. The light lunches offer unusual soups, with perhaps a hot cheese and bacon scone, pates and salads. In the evening tomato & mint soup, spring lamb with a gooseberry sauce, followed by fresh raspberries & shortbread, a selection of local cheeses and homemade petit fours & coffee is a typical delicious example. Elizabeth favours the unpretentious excellence of Elisabeth Ayrton's traditional recipes, many of which are in this book, adapting them according to what is locally available. This is certainly one of the most interesting and enjoyable eating experience in the country.

Still in Bridge Street we find the home of the Berwick Cockle in Mr Cowe's grocers shop. This is a lovely building with an elegant, if weather-beaten facade. The business was begun in 1801 by a Mr Weatherhead and taken over by William Cowe and Son, "Tea Dealers, Family Grocers and Italian Ware-housmen". The interior of the shop is virtually unchanged and the huge lacquered chests which held the tea are still behind the counter.

The red and white striped peppermint sweet, shaped like a cockle, has remained popular for over a hundred years and is still sold in a small glass jar. Her Royal Highness, Princess May of Teck, was a great fan and allowed them a royal warrant in 1886.

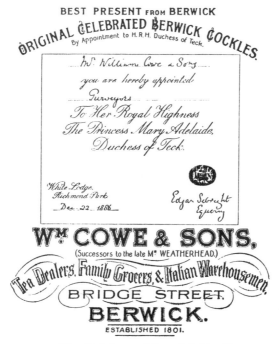

The Celebrated Berwick Cockle

Wm. Cowe & Sons

We now cross the beautiful old bridge, dominated by the more recent Royal Tweed Bridge and the wonderful railway viaduct. Look out for seals in the river, as they often swim up to find salmon. Sometimes they are successful and can be seen bobbing about with a huge fish, trying to avoid the hungry seagulls which dive bomb them in the hope of an easy snack.

Cross the main road onto the A698 and take the first right towards Horncliffe, following the signs for the Union Bridge. This is a glorious bit of engineering suspended over the River Tweed. Thomas Telford studied it before embarking on plans for the Menai Bridge. Completed in 1820 it symbolised the Union between England and Scotland having a rose motif on one end and thistle on the other and the hopeful motto "Stronger in Unity".

Union Bridge, Horncliffe

12

Overlooking the river is Willie and Daphne Robson's Chain Bridge Honey Farm. This is a unique and exceptionally well put together enterprise. Happily, it is now open to the public every day from April 1st, weekends only November to Christmas. It is a must for anyone remotely interested in beekeeping. The displays and observation hives would intrigue children and there is also the chance to buy honey, beeswax cosmetics, candles and furniture polish from their ever growing range of bee based produce.

Historically, Northumberland is a beekeeping county. Perhaps because of its extensive heather moorland. In the Bronze Age honey was widely used in medicine as well as in food and drink. The wax was, however, the most valuable product, being used in the "lost wax" method of bronze casting, where the wax melts from the mould during the process.

The Romans were particularly fond of it and introduced many sophisticated honey recipes. In Saxon times it was sometimes used to pay the rent. In medieval England, every monastery had its own apiary. The monks loved the clear flame and mellow light that only beeswax candles can give. They were also partial to their mead. The monks of Lindisfarne kept their hives on the mainland at Beal, Bee hill, to supply their needs.

According to Willie, the coastal plain running up to Berwick was a bee paradise of white clover pastures until the 1930's when intensive arable farming gradually took over. Following his father Selby, a lecturer, adviser and respected authority on beekeeping throughout the border counties, Willie has spent the last twenty years building up to 1,000 hives.

With the introduction of the early flowering yellow Rape, the bees can be buzzing as early as April. White clover then provides food until the hives are moved out onto the moors near Chatton and Rothbury. At the end of the season the bees are taken to sheltered winter sites and the honey brought back to the farm to be processed at the farm. All this is explained by Anne Middleditch, a knowledgeable and experienced beekeeper who runs the beautifully presented education centre. This is a mellow wood panelled room, scented by beeswax, full of pictures, displays, models and information to fascinate all ages.

Pure heather honey is so special that some hives are strategically placed to ensure that their diet is gleaned mainly from this source. The Robson's honey is superb and there are all different kinds to try. It is really too good to cook with but does give a marvellous flavour to all kinds of recipes.

Honey Cakes

1 lb honey	*A pinch of ground cloves*
1/4 lb butter	*pinch of salt*
1 lb flour	*$^1/_4$ oz bicarbonate soda*
1/4 lb ground almonds	*Grated rind of a lemon*

Sieve flour, salt and bicarb into a bowl. Add almonds and lemon rind and make a well in centre. Melt butter and honey and pour into centre of dry ingredients. Mix until well blended. Cover and allow to stand overnight. Next day sprinkle paste with a little flour. Roll out to 1/2" thickness and place on greased tin. Brush with lightly beaten white of egg and sprinkle with chopped almonds. Bake in a moderate over for 15 minutes until firm to the touch and pale brown.

Bee Wine

3 lbs honey	*1/2 oz yeast*
Peel of two lemons	*$^1/_4$ oz phosphate of ammonia*
1 gal. cold water	*3/4 oz cream of tartar*

Add honey and lemon peel to water and boil for 30 minutes. Pour into a container and when tepid, add the yeast creamed with a little cold water. Add phosphate and cream of tartar. Cover with muslin and leave to ferment. When liquid has ceased "working" cover container closely. Leave for six months then bottle and cork well.

A once thatched cottage in Horncliffe Village is said to have sheltered Oliver Cromwell when his army crossed the Tweed at the nearby ford and set up camp on their way to Berwick. A walk past the old mill and into Horncliffe Dene with its variety of wild plants makes a pleasant break.

Horncliffe Mill, 1880

Continuing on this minor road we come to the romantic ruins of Norham Castle, perched high above the Tweed. It was a favourite subject with Victorian artists, including Turner who made many sketches here. Norham was never a fairy tale castle, having for centuries been at the centre of some of the most desperate and bloody border battles.

Sir Walter Scott in his epic poem "Marmion" describes:

Day set on Norham's castled steep
And Tweeds fair river broad and deep
And Cheviot's mountain lone.
The battled towers, the donjon keep,
The loophole grates where captives weep.
The flanking walls around it sweep
In yellow lustre shone.

It was built in 1122 to deter Scots invasion, as was everything along the Tweed, and suffered under many a siege. In 1327 the garrison held a feast to celebrate the coronation of Edward III. They were so intent on their eating and drinking that they nearly fell prey to a horde of hungry Scots who were lurking in the vicinity.

In 1496 the great canon "Mons Meg" was hauled down from Edinburgh to blast the castle into submission. However the brave Bishop Fox, a prelate in the David Jenkins mould, held the enemy at bay for sixteen long days until help arrived. Battles were often won or lost in those days according to who had the most food. An efficient quartermaster was vital to success. Norham would have been filled with flour and ale, keeping cattle and sheep within its outer wall.

Norham Castle

Border knights in the best boy scout tradition were always prepared. Much to the surprise and possibly, derision of their southern counterparts, they always carried their own bag of flour and a bakestone attached to their saddles so that they could make their oatcakes and bannocks wherever they camped. Being a canny race perhaps they just didn't want to pay over the odds for their buns.

Oatmeal Cakes

1 oz bacon fat,
dripping or butter scant
1/4 pt water

4 oz coarse oatmeal
^{3}/4 *tspn salt*
^{3}/4 *tspn bicarbonate of soda*

Heat the fat with the water until it melts. Stir together the oatmeal, salt and bicarbonate. Add the liquid and mix to a stiff paste. Form into eight balls, squash flat and press more oatmeal onto each side. They should be about ^{1}/2*"* *thick. Cook on both sides on a greased griddle, hotplate or frying pan or bake at 350F for 30 minutes.*

The Tweed at Norham is one of the best stretches for salmon fishing in the country. In recognition of the fishes contribution to the local economy, the medieval village cross in Norham is topped by a weather vane in the form of a salmon.

The church is one of the oldest in the county dating back to 831 when the Bishop of Lindisfarne dedicated it to Peter, Cuthbert and Ceolwulf. The latter became a king of Northumbria and made his mark by allowing the monks to drink wine and ale instead of their customary milk and water.

16

Back on the A698 the road passes the single arch of Twizel Bridge, where James IV, on a bad day, allowed the English artillery to cross unmolested on their way to victory at Flodden. The impressive Gothic pile next to it is an uncompleted folly built at the whim of Sir Francis Blake in 1770.

A little upstream the remains of a tiny chapel dedicated to St Cuthbert are just visible. Here was stored the venerated stone boat which carried the body of St Cuthbert from Melrose to Tilmouth before being taken to its final resting place in Durham. A local farmer, typically down to earth, decided that it was the very thing to pickle his beef in and decided to remove it. Legend has it that this did not suit the Saint who came in the night and broke it.

Pickled Beef

4-6 lb piece of brisket or sil-	*2 ozs saltpetre*
verside	*1 bayleaf*
7pts water	*1 sprig thyme*
$1^1/_2$ lbs coarse salt	*10 crushed juniper berries*
1 lb dark brown sugar	*10 crushed peppercorns*

Put all brine ingredients in a pan and boil hard for five minutes. Strain into a crock or bucket and leave to cool. Immerse the meat and leave for at least seven to ten days. To cook the beef, rinse it or soak overnight in clean water. Put in pan. Cover with water add onion stuck with cloves, herbs and seasoning, sliced carrots. Bring to boil, cover and simmer. Allow thirty minutes per pound and thirty minutes over. Can be eaten hot or cold.

Bypassing Cornhill the A697 leads to Crookham where the last border skirmish took place in 1678. Half way between the two villages is a seven foot high stone said to mark the spot where James IV fell in battle. It is locally known as the Gathering Stone from the days when it was a rallying spot for local men in times of war.

Turning left onto the B6354 we come to the model villages of Ford and Etal, part of the 15,000 acre Joicey Estate. Here Lord Joicey and his marketing manager Fergus Waters continue to implement the progressive ideas to improve the estate. This involves carefully planned tourist strategy which enhances the existing buildings and provides interest and employment for local people.

Heatherslaw Mill has certainly been given a new lease of life. Corn has been ground on this site for over a thousand years. The mill which was extensively restored in the eighteenth century is now the centre of three thriving businesses. From Easter each year it is open to the public who can watch the milling process from beginning to end, looking down onto the huge mill wheel as it thunders round in the race.

The manager John Bradley now produces up to fifteen tons of flour a year. Most of the grain, wheat, barley, oats and rye are grown locally, some of it organic. Anyone with a small amount of special grain is welcome to bring it to Heatherslaw to have it milled.

Packed in strong paper bags all the different flours are sold in the mill shop along with their De Luxe Muesli which seems to contain every nut and grain known to man. Oat, wheat, barley and rye flakes are combined with brazils, hazelnuts, roasted peanuts, walnuts and sunflower seeds among other things. Several shops in the area sell these products and the flour is used in large quantity by specialist bakers.

Next door to the mill, Marion Middleton provides delicious fare for the visitors in the Granary Cafe. Colin Smurthwaite is also busy cooking at the Heatherslaw Bakery. This new business uses flour from the mill and produces a range of cakes and biscuits. All are made to traditional recipes and from local ingredients. At present there are Date and Walnut, Farmhouse Fruit and Cherry and Raisin Cakes plus butter and chocolate chip shortbreads, ginger parkin and oatmeal and coconut crunch. Four staff are employed and Colin and his wife are kept busy delivering.

18

Visiting Etal village on a quiet summers day is rather like experiencing a time warp back to almost any time you like. The castle ruins date back to the fourteenth century. The black mass of the gate-house and keep show what a formidable building it must have been, standing sentinel to protect the strategically important ford over the River Till.

Like Ford and Chillingham Castle, Etal was built on a quadrangle enclosing a vast courtyard. When excavations were made some years ago a vast kitchen was unearthed, lined with stone troughs and slab tables. Unfortunately it had to be filled in again for safety. One can imagine the hard worked staff of Lord Robert de Manners turning spits and basting great sides of venison. Only men were employed in big kitchens like this. Probably because everything was so heavy to carry. What couldn't be roasted was cooked in cauldrons over a blazing fire. Boy scullions who lived in the kitchen did all the menial work, cleaning the spits and ladles.

Etal Keep

The wide village street is more Victorian in style, with its picturesque gardens and one or two thatched roofs like The Black Bull run by Tom and Beryl Hails. A summer bar lunch here might consist of a Northumbrian stottie, a big, flat bread bun filled with Holy Island crabmeat, or homemade pate from Ann Walton's farmshop at Roseden and in the evenings baked Tweed Salmon with garden vegetables.

Etal Manor is an elegant Georgian house, now the home of Lord Joicey and his family and next to it is the church of St Mary.

Ford is also an anachronism and has been aptly described as "Chippendale gothic". Its Victorian gentility and uniformity are strangely out of place in the middle of wild Northumberland. However, as an exercise in planning a community it was eminently successful.

Ford Castle

Ford School 1900

The author of this scheme was Louisa, the lovely Marchioness of Waterford who came to live at Ford Castle on her marriage in 1842. The castle was originally the manor of Odinel de Forde and was fortified 1338 by Sir William Heron. It was destroyed and rebuilt several times before Lady Louisa put her Victorian stamp on it.

When her husband died, all Louisa's energy was channelled into rebuilding among the mature trees in the castle grounds. Here a score of houses, a post office, Estate House, Blacksmith's shop and a school came into being, surrounded by gardens now overflowing with clematis and roses.

The school is perhaps the most interesting building. Two fine fig trees give shelter to the schoolroom, the interior walls of which are covered in biblical murals painted by the Marchioness. She was an independent lady, intelligent and gifted and a close associate of the notorious Pre Raphaelitte brotherhood of artists that included Dante Gabriel Rossetti, Holman Hunt and Millais among their number. Her work echoes their clarity and bright colours. She used people from the estate as her models and local people can still see the pictures of their great grandparents painted when they were children over a hundred years ago.

The school is open to the public and it is also possible to enjoy a superb lunch here thanks to the good ideas and hard work of Olivia Mason who has recently started offering "Food at Ford".

Olivia, who is a farmer's wife from Crookham, won an English Tourism Award for excellence and the Daily Express Countrywoman of the Year for her catering skills. She still finds time to whip up gourmet dinner parties and wedding breakfasts as well as providing lunch in the Waterford Hall for groups of thirty or more who are visiting the area. She uses the best and most unusual produce in the area, especially a wide variety of game and seafood. A sample lunch might consist of cream of vegetable soup with a Heatherslaw bread roll followed by casserole of Venison or Crown Roast of Lamb with apple stuffing.

21

Venison Stew

2 lbs Venison	rind of a lemon
3 oz dripping	2 tbspns wine vinegar
2 tbspns flour	1 pt hot stock or red wine
seasoning	2 tbspns redcurrant jelly
2 tbspns chopped onion	

Cut meat into 1" pieces. Toss in flour seasoned well with salt, pepper and a little nutmeg. Melt fat, when smoking add meat and onion, turn in pan until well browned. Add liquid and stir until well mixed. Cover pan and cook slowly on hotplate or in over for about two hours until meat is tender. Add redcurrant jelly and lemon rind and season again. Reheat before serving.

Leaving Ford on the B6353 take the B6525 to Berwick which passes through Ancroft. This little village was once a busy centre for boot and clog making and shod Marlborough's army. Plague decimated the population in 1667 and there is still a field called Broomie Huts in memory of the area where the victims were carried and left under shelters made from broom. As they died the broom provided a bier for their cremation. A line of trees on the left of the road was planted in their memory, one for each clogger.

The Norman church was first built by the Holy Island monks in 1145 and was fortified in the fourteenth century to make it a safe refuge from the Scots.

The vicarage and its outbuildings, according to one archdeacon's plans, was said to have been for some reason capable of receiving two hundred children and under the same roof provide "comfortable habitation for the curate". Poor curate!!

At the next crossroads is Oxford Farm with its well stocked farm shop. Here Maureen Brown sells every jam, marmalade and chutney you can name and a delicious range of homemade scones and cakes. In season there are fresh raspberries and strawberries.

At the main road we turn left to return to Berwick for a feast of fish at the Rob Roy restaurant in Dock Road, Tweedmouth. The emphasis here is on providing the best ingredients enhanced, rather than drowned by simple, well flavoured sauces. Featured in the Telegraph Eating Out guide and awarded Best Seafood Pub of the Year, the owners Keith and Julie Wilson work hard to vary their excellent menu.

In the Salmon Company Bar you can choose from crab, prawn, smoked or fresh salmon sandwiches. Pickled herrings and Lindisfarne oysters need no accompaniment or perhaps a grilled lemon sole, smoked trout or half a lobster with salad depending on the season.

22

The evening menu is even more mouth-watering. The Seafood platter for two might include lobster, smoked salmon and prawns and four or five other shellfish depending what is best at that time of year.

Northumbrian lobster is always very popular, lightly grilled with garlic or gently casseroled with locally grown asparagus and butter sauce. Salmon from the Berwick Salmon Company is always available and is offered poached in a sparkling white wine or simply grilled.

Although the fish and seafood are undoubtedly the main attraction here there is always a selection of good border steaks, game or local duckling. A worthy end to our browse round Berwick and the Border.

Rob Roy's Lindisfarne Oysters in a Cream Sauce

Steam open half a dozen oysters per person in a little dry white wine. Remove from shells, retaining the deep bottom shell. Strain liquid of any debris and reserve. In a knob of butter lightly fry finely chopped shallots. Do not brown them. Add the strained liquor and add a little more wine. Reduce to two or three tbspns strongly flavoured stock. Add the oysters and enough double cream to cover them. Bring gently to the boil. Add chopped parsley and season. Serve immediately in the warmed shells.

23

The Boy in Lady Waterford Hall

Trail Two
Coquetdale
Shepherds
Pie

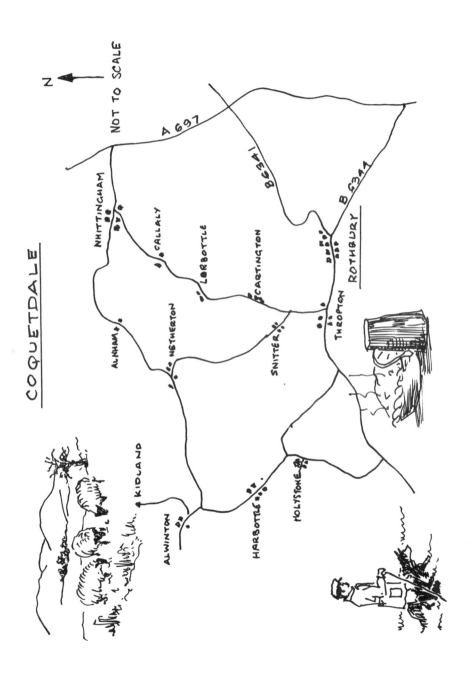

Coquetdale Shepherd's Pie

Rothbury Mart, Cira 1900

Good luck to the Hoof and the Horn
Good Luck to the Flock and the Fleece
Good Luck to the growers of Corn
With the blessings of Plenty and Peace

This poem, written above the ring in Rothbury Mart sets the scene for our next trail. As it winds through the hills and valleys of the Coquet and Whittingham Vale, it passes some of the best stock rearing farms in the county. Cattle and sheep provide not only a living but a whole way of life to the farmers. Traditions continue in these valleys giving a taste of rural Northumberland, untouched by time.

Rothbury, where we begin, has always been a popular spot with tourists. The Romans, Vikings, Norman barons and most frequently the Scots, who galloped through the "debatable lands" at the head of the Coquet to bring back a plump sheep or plumper local maiden as a souvenir, have sampled the town's hospitality in one way or another.

Providing food, shelter and "in house" entertainment seems to be a long-standing tradition and in the early 1700's Rothbury boasted seven hostelries,

27

including the Three Half Moons' where the Earl of Derwentwater and his Jacobite supporters stayed in 1715.

The tired traveller could choose form "The Malt Shovel", The Golden Fleece, Fox and Hounds, Black Bull, The Rifleman or if he fancied a bit of local colour, "the Fighting Cocks" named for the five thriving cock pits in the vicinity. Bull baiting was also recorded in the 1720's.

Feeding the ducks on the river is more popular with modern visitors, but sport still plays a large part in the lives of the "natives" and hunting, shooting and fishing thrive in the valley.

The river Coquet has long been a famous fishing river and salmon and more often, trout are regularly on the local menu. In 1834 a fishing party staying at the "Black Bull", enjoyed the cooking of Mrs burns, the proprietors wife, who treated them to "a dish of hotch potch, a piece of salmon and a saddle of Cheviot mutton" while deciding whether to use the "black hackle" or the "Midge fly".

Hotch Potch

"An emblem o' the hail vegetable and animal creation". Saute chopped spring onions, cauliflower, carrots, turnips, peas and beans. Add to stock made from neck of Lamb, with the meat from the bone and simmer till tender. Season and serve. Any combination of seasonal vegetable can be used for this "lusty" broth.

The most prized fish to catch at that time was the willy "skegger", a large bull trout which knew how to "skeg" or seek cover in the shadow of the bank or rock and which were sometimes called "alter" "alder troots" as they hid under the roots of the alder tree making the sport more challenging! If the catching is complicated, the cooking is simple.

Baked Trout

2 River Trout	*1 tspn capers*
Seasoning 1oz butter	*Lemon juice*
Bread crumbs	

Clean fish and lay head to tail on greased, fireproof dish. Sprinkle with salt, pepper, lemon juice and roughly chopped capers. Put a light cover of bread-crumbs over all and lay on butter in small pieces. Cover in greased paper and bake in a moderate oven for 15-20 mins. serve hot with slices of lemon.

Good food has always been important to Rothbury folk and in the 1800's when visitors flocked here from the town to sample the goat's milk and whey for which it was famous, there were fourteen grocer's shops to cater for the needs of Lord and labourer.

The best known of these was Dixons at the West end of the village, which specialised in unusual teas and coffees, roasting their own blend behind the shop. This was owned by the family of "Dippie "Dixon, better known for his marvellous books on local history. Dippie himself owned a drapers shop at Coquetdale House." R. Pagon, "Dealer in Feeding Stuffs" had a smart pony and cart to deliver his goods and the East end of the village was supplied by the Davidson family.

Tullys. C1900

Today Edwin and Mary Tully, whose family were one of those fourteen, maintain the tradition in their excellent shop in the middle of the high street. This is no impersonal megastore but a haven of old fashioned courtesy led by

Clive Harrison and his assistants who will point out interesting new treats to try. These range from locally produced cheeses, home cured hams and herb flavoured sausages, eggs, local vegetables and preserves as well as the usual range of fare expected from a first class grocer.

Fresh bread, cakes, pies and biscuits are available from two bakeries. Howard Philips "Greenwell Bakery" operates from the site of the original village bakehouse at Townfoot. Here Howard bravely rises at crack of dawn to make his bread, cakes and pies. The meat pies, made with beef from R. Green , in Longhorsley are great favourites with the natives of Rothbury.

The "Home Bakery" run by Arthur and Jeanette Middleton uses Heatherslaw Mill's stoneground wholemeal flour for some of their bread and also supplies Heatherslaw's tasty range of biscuits, Willie Robson's "Chain Bridge" honey and an excellent choice of cold meats, beef, pork, ham and turkey, all reared in the county, and cooked in huge joints on the premises. These can be made up into buns to be taken away and in season fresh crab is also an option. Accompanied by a bottle of "Cheviot Castle" spring water bottled at source by the Murray family at nearby Cartington, this provides the basis of a good picnic for the ever increasing flow of hungry visitors.

If coffee and homemade biscuits are preferred the "Sun Kitchen", owned and run by Heather Easton, is a good place to sit and look down onto the tree lined Market place and Church .

Two miles West of Rothbury lies Thropton, also known as "Tattie Toon", supposedly because it was the best place in the valley to grow potatoes. An old villager once said that "It was ne use onybody gan to leeve at Thropton if they cuddent taak aboot taties". One can only imagine the intense and excited exchange in the local hostelries about the merits of Maris Pilot v King Edwards, and whispered conversations about "blight" and "rot" between husband and wife from the privacy of their bedrooms!

30

Pan Haggerty

2 lb potatoes cut into slices   *6 ozs grated cheese*
1 lb sliced onions   *salt and pepper*
1 tbspn dripping

Place the layers of potato,onion and cheese in a heavy pan containing the hot dripping. Season each layer and fry until browned. Cover with a lid and cook until the potatoes are tender. This can be served in its own or with meat.

That Thropton is still the centre of vegetable and indeed, other excellence, can be seen at their annual Show in August. Here the aptly named Industrial Tent is filled with local produce. From the ubiquitous "tattie" to the best stand of identical carrots and onions; from the lightest sponge cake or brownest egg or most jewel-coloured jelly to the most potent elderflower wine or fruit packed cake.

Countrymen and women in this area still scorn the temptations of M & S for the satisfaction of growing or baking their own, infinitely tastier fare. Here recipes are passed down from mother to daughter.

Northumbrian Farmhouse Fruit Cake

4 ozs mixed fruit4ozs caster   *(Earl Grey gives a lovely*
sugar   *flavour)*
^{1}/4 hot strong tea   *1 egg*
2 tbspns chunky marmalade   *8 ozs self raising flour*

Place fruit, sugar and tea in a bowl. Leave to stand for at least six hours. Add the marmalade and beaten egg, sieve in the flour and mix well. Turn into a greased 1lb loaf tin and bake at 350F for 50-60 minutes.

In an area of farmers and foresters where so many work on the land or indulge in strenuous outdoor hobbies, there is still a need for substantial home cooked food. A heavy days dipping, clipping or lambing will not be sustained on a pre-packed duck breast or prawn vol au vent, however delicious. "Real men" need real food and although our jaded palates can experience exotic delicacies from all over the world, all year round, there is still nothing more enjoyable or companionable than seeing, smelling and consuming a feast of home steak and kidney pie, garden potatoes and a simple apple tart, baked in the Aga and eaten round the kitchen table after a hard day's work.

Thropton and surrounding villages also had a need to be self sufficient because of the threat of Scottish invasion which might leave them isolated for weeks in times of unrest. In the middle of the village the "lytle toure of the inherytaunce of Sir Cuthbert Ratclyffe, Knighte" now converted to a house, was in 1509 garrisoned 16 soldiers to protect the village.

Food in those days was simple, seasonal and monotonous. Meat was only eaten on special occasions by the ordinary folk, whose staples were bread, vegetables and occasionally, cheese. Even farmers with their own beef and lamb had to eat cured, pickled and dried meat for half the year. "From Christmas to May, weak cattle decay" and as there was no winter fodder until the root crops of the late 18th century, all non breeding stock were fattened and killed in November. huge hooks in the beams of the oldest houses in the area testify to the hanging of vast sides of meat.

Genuine travellers as opposed to savage marauders, have always been welcome in Thropton and there is evidence of two ancient "hospitals". One on the site of Wreighburn House, which was once known as Thropton Spital. This was thought to belong to the ancient order of the Knights of St John of Jerusalem. The other was just across the river at Allerdene and called the Rye Hill Spital. Both these sites were on major highways which were later used as drove roads for shepherds bringing their stock to sell in Rothbury or farther afield.

Such hospitals provided food, shelter and medical help for pilgrims, travellers and the needy of the parish. Physic Lane in Thropton is probably the site of the gardens where the hospitallers grew their herbs for cooking and remedies. Two hostelries, The Three Wheat Heads and The Cross Keys provide food and drink for the weary, who hopefully have no need for the medicine.

Regular Customers

The road to Harbottle passes some of the best farmland in the area. Warton for example, was noted by Dippie Dixon as having a "super excellence of soil". The substantial stone built farm steading, now owned by the National Trust, is a monument to the standards of husbandry practised by generations of competent farmers. In 1835 the then owner, Robert Spearman was awarded a silver cup by his friends for his feat in producing the famous "Warton Ox".

This noble beast was slaughtered on the 6th March, 1835, weighing an astounding 200 stones 6lbs! Before its demise, this Billy Bunter of the bullock world was taken round the border towns in a specially made trailer by his proud owner, in a tour de force of agricultural one upmanship. There is still a field at Warton, now farmed by the Davy family, called Great Ox Close in his memory.

Just before the hamlet of Sharperton lies a farm called Charity Hall, once owned by the parish to grow food for the Poorhouses in the area. A typical menu of the 1850's might consist of;
Breakfast: Hasty pudding and one gill of milk.
Lunch: Hashed meat or on Sundays, boiled beef or mutton.
Supper: Bread and milk or broth and bread.

It was said that "the food is of the best quality and those who prefer it may have good table beer for supper instead of milk". The sick and infirm were allowed tea and coffee. Occasionally there might be fish or offal and plum pudding or frumenty on special occasions. This seems a very adequate menu in the circumstances. It is an interesting statistic that the equivalent current government support falls short of the amount needed to provide an equally nutritious diet.

Hasty Pudding

$1^{1}/_{2}$ milk
1 oz sugar
$2^{1}/_{2}$ ozs ground rice or semolina.

Heat the milk almost to boiling point, sprinkle on ground rice or semolina, stirring briskly, lower heat and simmer until grain is cooked and mixture begins to thicken. Add sugar and stir. This might sound very dull but if served with cream and jam or treacle is really very good and couldn't be easier.

Once over Sharperton bridge a detour of half a mile finds the tiny village of Holystone, an oasis of pretty cottages and gardens tucked under high "Haremoor Law". The steepness of the roofs suggests that many of the houses would at one time have been heather thatched. Such dwellings were extremely simple, consisting of two rooms separated by box beds with sliding doors. The

mattresses were filled with oat chaff and there was no heating apart from a small fire and the warmth from the house.

A well known inhabitant of the village in the 1820's was Ned Allan, a weaver by trade but a fisherman by inclination. He was famous for his skill with the "five tailed teister". This was a lethal weapon for catching eels, which were then plentiful in the Coquet and were a welcome addition to the local diet. When Ned died, the village schoolmaster wrote:

Here lies Ned in his cold bed,
For hunting otters famed.
A faithful friend lies by his side,
and "Tug'em" he was named.
Sport and rejoice, ye finny tribes
That glide in Coquet river,
Your deadly foe no more you'll see,
For he is gone for ever.

Eels are now considered an expensive delicacy, but were once common fare for Northumbrians and could be cooked in a variety of ways.

Mrs Allgoods Collared Eals

Skin your eals and slit them down the back. Take out the bone, then take sage, parsley, shred small and salt and season them well. Role them up in your hand and boil them half an hour in the water and white wine vinegar with salt, whole pepper, mace and sweet herbs. When they are drained and cold keep them in the liquor til they are served.

The Salmon Inn in the centre of the village was a well known haunt for anglers from far and wide. One enthusiastic fisherman wrote in 1780 that he left Rothbury at four in the morning and fished his way up the Coquet, arriving at the Salmon at eight. Just in time for breakfast. He feasted on "old Dame B's barley cake and new milk" and for dinner there was bacon and eggs, old milk, cheese, barley cake and new butter and best malt whiskey mixed with water from Lady's Well.

This all sounds very civilised but the author of "Rambles in Northumberland" wrote in 1835 "A person who is fastidiously nice has no business in Holystone". How intriguing!

Barley Bread

This was made fresh every day, often with flour ground in the village, which was the case at Holystone. The meal can still be bought at Heatherslaw Mill. It is best served hot from the oven.

$1^{1/}{}_2$ lbs barley flour　　　　*pinch of bicarbonate of soda*
lard the size of a pullets egg　　　*buttermilk or soured*
1 tspn cream of tartar　　　　　*milk..........good pinch of salt*

Rub the fat into the flour and salt. Mix cream of tartar and bicacb with a little warm milk. Add to flour and add enough milk to make a soft dough. Form into a round about 3/4 thick with the hands and mark lightly into sections. Cook on a floured tray in a medium oven until brown and crumbly.

As its name suggests Holystone has a strong religious history and before the Reformation was the site of a Benedictine Priory and home to a handful of hardy nuns. All that remains of their time here is a field called "Nun's Close" and one or two huge stones which mark the foundations of their church.

Nun's Biskett

(This is a very old recipe which sounds rather indulgent for a nun)

Take a pound of fine sugar, half a pound of almonds beaten with orange flower water and eight eggs. Beat all together until it be very white. Put in a quarter of a pound of flour, well dried, the rind of two lemons and beat well. Butter and dredge your pans. Bake all these things together in a quick oven.

The tranquil "Lady's Well" can be reached by crossing a plank bridge over the stream behind the pub. A thick grove of trees protects the stone lined pool

35

where a fountain of bright spring water rises. In the centre stands a lichened stone cross which tells us that "In this place Paulinus, the Bishop, baptised three thousand Northumbrians. Easter DCXXVII." At one end of the pool a weathered stone figure keeps watch and in the summer evenings tiny pipistrelle bats flit in and out of the trees, catching insects and swooping to sip from the pool. There is always an atmosphere of almost magical calm in this very holy place.

Harbottle, unlike the cosy cluster of Holystone, has one long main street the Star Inn, the Doctors surgery and the Village Hall being the most important social centres. The inhabitants, like their forebears, are mainly involved in farming and forestry.

In the 1870's the doctor wrote a letter to the "Times" on the hardiness and longevity of his patients. This was due to the "plain, substantial food, excellent water and regular work in a bracing atmosphere." This resulted in their being "highly intelligent and generally abstemious".

The food would have been produced by the villagers themselves. Most houses had vegetable gardens and room for a pig and chickens. The more outlying farms were supplied with other essentials by Pagon the grocer who had shops in Thropton and Rothbury. His horse and cart delivered goods and took farm eggs, butter, wild rabbits and other fare in exchange.

Pagon the Grocer

36

Before Winter set in a carrier would bring enough dry goods to last until the bad weather was over, often not until March. One family might need a hundredweight of flour. a chest of tea. Half a gallon of whisky in a big earthenware "grey hen" was also a must to keep out the cold.

The village water supply of which the doctor was so proud, was piped from a collecting tank high on Harbottle Hill. According to one local, it frequently collected dead sheep, moles and other flora and fauna. Perhaps this accounts for its special properties.

At one time Harbottle had a weekly market where local produce would be bought and sold. There was also an annual fair where the farmers, shepherds and drovers, who hardly saw a soul from one year to the next and had become rather wild and hairy, ventured down from the hills with their equally hairy and possibly wilder cattle and sheep. The two public houses, The Unicornand The Ship did big business and the release of a years pent up excitement or a harboured grudge often ended in a monumental brawl. Usually Coquetdale V Redesdale. When things were rather quiet one year a local remarked in great disappointment that "Its eleven o'clock i the fornyun an nivver a blow struck yet!"

Leaving the village, the manse and Parsonside hill are on the left. the hill is locally known for its wide variety of wild mushrooms and toadstools. There are three thousand species of fungi in Britain and only twenty or so are really poisonous and four fatally so. The sensible thing would be to learn which these were, still leaving a terrific choice.

At one time only priests were allowed to use them, perhaps because the properties of the more "magic" varieties led to visions. Having learnt what is safe, pick only on dry days into a big, wicker basket and cook them on the day of picking.

The Giant Puffball is quite common on Nothumbrian pastures. Make sure it is still firm and white. It can be cut into thick slices and fried in bacon fat or battered and fried. Alternatively it can be hollowed in the middle and the pieces mixed with minced bacon. herbs and seasoning, returned to the puffball, wrapped in foil and baked in the oven.

Harbottle Castle, overlooking the village was built by James IV and sheltered Henry VIII's sister, Margaret Tudor when she gave birth to the future mother of Lord Darnley, and mother in law of Mary Queen of Scots

High above the castle stands the Drake Stone. There is a lovely, but very steep walk up to these crags behind which lies the mysterious and remote Harbottle Lough. On a stormy day when the slate grey surface is rippled by the wind it is the perfect setting for Keat's ghostly poem "La Belle Dame Sans Merci" where the "sedge is withered from the lake and no birds sing".

The Drake Stone, apart from commanding glorious views, was very useful in times past as it provided the community with millstones and it is still obvious where they have been hewn out of the rock. This was a wild and wooded area hundreds of years ago and it is believed that the last wolf in England was killed near Harbottle Peels.

The Hamlet of Alwinton has always been something of a "frontier" settlement. It is still the last bit of civilisation before venturing into the "debatable" land where the Scottish raiders "sought the beeves that made their broth". The canny Scots usually waited until September or October to make their sorties, just as the cattle were properly fattened for slaughter in November.

Lying at the confluence of Alwin and the Coquet, Alwinton has always been a popular fishing spot. In the 1800's two inns, The Red Lion, run with an iron hand by Hannah Jordon, and The Rose and Thistle, had a steady flow of customers. Today only the Rose and Thistle, run by the Foreman family, survives, having been an inn for over three hundred years.

The Rose and Thistle, Alwinton

The pub and the church are very important in such an isolated place but what really holds this community together is the sheep and the culture that revolves around them. Everyone in the area is involved either with the great annual sheep show, the Shepherds's Suppers or the West Percy and Border Hunts, who strive to keep the wily hill fox numbers down in order to protect the lambs that are born "out by".

'Allanton' Show, as it is locally known is usually held in mid September, when the valley is all brown and gold. Despite the influx of visitors from the town, desperate for a bit of rustic charm, this is still very much a sheep show. The best animals from the Coquet and the Rede are dressed, indulged and paraded. Their faces are washed and whitened and their fleeces tinted and trimmed. Gentle rivalry is in order, unlike the disparaging verse penned by an earlier Coquet shepherd about his Redesdale counterpart.

Upper Redewitter for mosses and bogs
The main o' their leevin is tetties and hoggs
An if an aad ewe chance to dee of the rot
There's nae loss at her for she's guid for the pot

At one time the sheep was the main source of income and food. Mutton, rather than lamb was always on the menu in broths, stews or pies. Pies were perfected in medieval times and were useful because the pastry envelope allowed a great variety of ingredients to be combined, often fruit and meat together. It was also a convenient way of eating meat and gravy when knives were not in general use. For the farm labourer who took his "bait" to work, the pastry case was easy to carry and contained meat, vegetables and gravy in one sealed and tasty container.

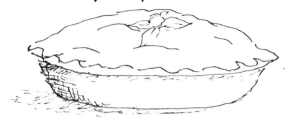

Mutton Pie

These pies will serve 8-10 hungry shepherds

2 lbs shortcrust pastry	*$^1/_2$ lb chopped onion*
$1^1/_2$ lbs lean mutton	*2 egg yolks*
$1^1/_2$ pts good thick gravy	*chopped parsley*
1oz butter	

Chop meat into 1/4 inch pieces. Heat butter and seal meat. Add onions and sautee quickly. Take off heat, add gravy and mix. Line deep patty with pastry. Fill with mutton mixture. Cover with pastry, crimp edges and make sure of hole in centre. Brush with egg yolks. Cook in moderate oven for 50-60 mins. Serve hot with chopped parsley.

The Annual Shepherd's Supper, according to Peter Wilson, who attends regularly, is a sort of pre-lambing binge. It takes place in early February in the Rose and Thistle. Here farmers and shepherds from miles around congregate to tell tales of nightmare lambings or unbelievable numbers of triplets and sing traditional and not so traditional shepherd's songs. It is a select gathering limited to 100. Tickets are sent to the favoured and if someone dies or is unable to come, his place is given to another eager soul.

Shepherd's Grace

O Lord, when hunger pinches sore,
Do thou stand us in stead,
And send us, from thy bounteous store,
A tup or wether Head!
Amen.

Burns.

Although a hearty supper is provided, the liquid refreshment is apparently of more importance. After the formal address to the Shepherds, given by a guest speaker, the serious business of jokes and songs take over.

A song much loved and regularly sung at these events is the "Canny Shepherd Laddies o" The Hills, written at the turn of the century by John Mowitt, a draper from Conway House, Rothbury. It is sung to the tune of "Keep your feet still, Geordie Hinny".

The Canny Shepherd Laddies O' The Hills

Noo wi all torn oot at Aalwinton
Tae see the Shepherd's Show,
Then into Foreman's for a drink
We wi wor cronies go.
They'll roar an shoot an dance an sing,
But fight, God Bless ya',no.
That's the canny shepherd laddies o' the hills.

O' the shepherds of the Coquet,
Of the Alwin and the Rede,
The Beaumont and the Breamish,
They are aal the same breed.
Wi' their collie dog beside them
and their stick with a horned heed
That's the canny shepherd laddies o' the hills.

If this seems a strictly male affair, the women of the Coquet have a more than supportive role over the centuries, nurturing orphan lambs and providing vast meals for the gangs at clipping, dipping and harvest. Hannah Hutton, herself a lovely singer of Northumbrian songs, wife of now retired shepherd Joe the acclaimed player of the Northumbrian pipes, remembers how hard it was. Four huge meals a day were expected by the fifteen hungry men who came to help. Traditional recipes come into their own at times like this.

Clipping Pudding

1 lb short grain rice	*pinch nutmeg*
2 pts creamy milk	*6 tbspns sugar*
8 ozs currants	*2 tbspns butter*
8 ozs raisins	*1 beaten egg*
tspn cinnamon	*pinch salt*

Put rice in pan with milk, spices and sugar. Simmer until cooked. Stir in eggs, fruit, butter and salt. Pour into a greased dish and bake in moderate oven for 20 minutes. Serves 15-20.

Farm Pound Cake

If any room was left after consuming the pudding this substantial fruit cake would fill the hungriest shepherd.

1 lb flour   *Grated rind and juice*
2 level tspns baking powder   *1 lb sultanas*
pinch salt   *1 lb sugar*
4 ozs glace cherries   *1 lb butter*
3 ozs chopped peel   *8 eggs*
2 lemons.

Beat butter and sugar, add rest of ingredients and a little milk if too stiff. Bake in a slow oven for 21/4-3hrs. Checking regularly.

Opposite the "Showfield" on the edge of the village is the Norman church of St Michael and the vicarage, which, like many border manses, was once a fortified bastle. This was no gentile parish and the vicar was often at the centre, if not the cause of many local disputes. In the thirteenth century the incumbent was pacified over a quarrel about tithes by an annual gift from the monks of Kidland. This strange backhander consisted of half a mark of silver, a pound of incense and a pound of pepper.

Pepper was at that time an extemely rare and valuable commodity, only available to the nobility or high ranking clergy. the venerable Bede recorded that his small allowance of pepper to flavour his food was one of his few and most precious possessions.

In the 1600's the vicar's pele was usurped by one troublesome John Hearon, who turned it into an alehouse, causing the vicar to build himself a tiny cottage out of his own "poor pension".

Crossing the river en route to Netherton a small road leads past Clennel Hall and up into the hills. At the turn of the century this isolated junction was a hive of social activity once a week when the grocer and the mail man came here to the "Alwin Market" to deliver their goods and take messages and farm produce back to the metropolis of Rothbury. All the local ladies dressed in their "good" clothes turned out to see their neighbours and have a gossip.

Alwin Hill Market

Further up the valley, looking out to Cheviot, the monks from Newminster Abbey built a monastery here in the thirteenth century. It must have been a very contemplative life as other than catching and cooking their meagre meals, there would be little to do. Even the possibility of bagging the odd pheasant or rabbit was denied them by the lord of the manor. He stopped their fun by insisting that they only keep three legged dogs, which would be unable to catch game.

The village of Netherton was known in its heyday for its "greyhound coursing, bachelor's balls, merry nights and social functions". The two inns, The Fighting Cocks' and the Star providing refreshments during these exciting events.

Mine Host at The Star in the 1800's was Walter Pattinson, also the local "eggler". With his sturdy pony adorned with creels or panniers he visited all the local farms collecting butter and eggs for resale. On one such trip he was treated to several drinks. the farmer, having winched Watty back onto his horse, caused him to put a foot in each basket. He then walloped the pony which set off for home at the speed of light. Arriving home, the legless Walter called happily to his wife. "Hi, Betty, come and see your Watty kirning!!".

If Betty was a typically thrifty Northumbrian lady, when she had sorted out the errant Walter, she might have salvaged what was left of the butter and eggs to make a herbolace, the forerunner of the scrambled egg. For this the butter was heated in a saucepan and eight well beaten eggs mixed with chopped herbs and ginger tossed into a pan.

It is possible that there were goose eggs in the creel as Coquetdale farmers traditionally reared geese. When they were fattened, instead of a sale there was a goose lottery. Here friends and neighbours of the farmer gathered in the farmhouse or a handy pub. Each goose was valued, stakes were made and a game of cards played, the winner taking the goose. This was often followed by songs, drink and a generous supper described as "just roast and boiled for ever and dumplins and puddens and then sic lashins o' drink". Village whist drives, sadly minus the goose, continue this tradition.

In the North country when there was a large family the "six legged goose" was a favourite to make ends meet. The goose proper was well stuffed with herbs and the thighs and legs of a rabbit. During cooking the rabbit joints take on the flavour of the goose. When the goose was served, the pieces of goosey rabbit were given to the smallest children who were supposed not to know the difference!

Geese were often given by tenants to their landlords at Michaelmas after they had been cheaply fattened on the grain stubbles.

And when the tenants come,to pay their quarters rent
They bring some fowls at midsummer
A dish of fish at Lent
At Christmas a capon, at Michaelmas a goose
And somewhat else at New Years Tide
For feare their lease flies loose

A few geese are still reared on local farms and sold from the premises or at the nearest mart where they always command a good price. In Victorian times goose was the preferred Christmas dinner, often accompanied by this next recipe.

North Country Savoury Pudding

$1^1/_4$ pts milk

$^1/_4$ lb fine oatmeal

$^1/_4$ breadcrumbs

2 eggs

3 ozs flour

$^1/_4$ lb suet

2 tbspns chopped sage,

thyme and parsley

$^1/_2$ lb chopped onion

pepper and salt

Heat milk and pour over bread and oatmeal. Mix suet, herbs, seasoning with flour. Add onions. Mix well with oatmeal. Add extra milk if needed. Bake for approx. 1 hour. Serve like Yorkshire pudding. This is also very good with roast pork.

The road from Netherton to Alnham leads into the "white grass" foothills on the southern side of Cheviot, only six miles from the Scottish border. Since the fourteenth century the village and much of the surrounding land has belonged to the Percy family and was originally a strongly fortified outpost with a pele tower, castle and church.

Looking after food, whether it was on the hoof or otherwise was a constant struggle. in 1532, three hundred Scots from Teviotdale ransacked the village removing "corne, hay and household stuf" and way down the list "also a woman", no doubt to do the cooking.

The owner of the tower, whether to safeguard his mutton supply or because he was overly fond of his sheep, according to a surveyor's report, took them "up the stares to lay them in his chambers, which rotteth the vaultes, and will in shorte time be the utter decay of the same house"

The glorious landscapes on this route exist because of the hill farmers efforts to preserve them. It is all too easy when complaining about the price of a Sunday joint to forget that the money, of which the farmer only gets a very small percentage, also contributes to maintaining rural Northumberland.

Not only do these farms provide food, they have always been the centre of rural tradition and culture. Prendwick for example, before the days of commercial markets, hosted one of the most important lamb sales in the country. It was also the venue for a Kirn Supper which the whole valley attended.

After the harvest was gathered into the stackyard, the word was spread to attend the party. The last sheaf from the last field was dressed as the "Kirn Dolly" and carried in procession to the barn where the feast was to take place. Tea and spice loaf was eaten first and pieces of cake into which had been baked a ring, a sixpence and a button. Whoever found one of these in their slice would either soon be married, rich but not loved or never married at all.

During the evening the fiddlers would arrive and the dancing begin. Guests were kept going with ale, bread, cheese and more cake until the early hours.

Kirn suppers are still held in village halls all over the county, supported mainly by the older generation who have followed the tradition all their lives and look forward to a good evening's "crack", followed by a dance to the local band.

Harvest Cake

8 ozs barley flour	*4 ozs sugar*
8 ozs plain flour	*1 tbspn golden syrup*
$1^1/_2$ tspns baking powder	*8 ozs sultanas*
$^1/_2$ tspn salt	*$^1/_2$ pt milk*
4 ozs butter	

Sift the two flours with baking powder and salt. Cream butter and sugar and add syrup. Add flour and milk alternately and mix well. Fold in sultanas. Put in a buttered 7" tin. Bake at 350F for 11/2 hours.

Overnight Spice Loaf

1 lb plain flour	*3 tspns mixed spice*
6 ozs lard	*$2^1/_2$ tspns Bicarbonate of soda*
2ozs butter	*8 ozs currants*
8 ozs sugar	*8 ozs raisins*
4 ozs ground almonds	*$^1/_2$ pt sour milk*

Rub the fat into the flour, sift in sugar, almonds, spice and soda. Scatter with fruit and mix with milk. Place in a lined, greased 8-9" tin nad leave overnight. Bake for 1 hour at 325F then 150F for a further hour.

Nearing Whittingham, the road skirts the parkland of Eslington Hall, home of the Ravensworth family. The elegant house is surrounded by landscaped grounds where a fold of toffee coloured Highland cattle always graze. An earlier Lord Ravensworth introduced a small herd of reindeer from Lapland to the estate in 1786 and a field at the Mountain Farm is still called "Reindeer Close".

Dippie Dixon, author of "Upper Coquetdale" and "Whittingham Vale" writes of his youthful treats at nearby Ryle Mill. The great yetlin or cauldron full of delicious oatmeal porridge, was always ready for hordes of helpers and the homemade cheese, curds, cream and "white cakes" and new butter which he helped to make.

Whittingham dates back to Saxon times and in 882 produced Cuthred who became King of Northumbria.

During the battles fought in the times of the Cavaliers and Roundheads, a troop of over four hundred of Cromwell's psalm singing supporters arrived in the village unannounced, demanding breakfast. They "behaved civilly and paid for everything". In the 1800's when Dixon's the grocers were rebuilding their seventeenth century house, they found an enormous oven where the loaves for the troops must have been baked.

Word must have travelled as only eight years later two hundred weary Cavaliers sought food and shelter but were captured by Roundheads without a fight.

Perhaps the three hostelries drew travellers. The best known was the "Hole in the Wall", which survives as a house just opposite the road junction to Glanton. The hostess was "Aad Syb Copeland".

If you ever go to Whittingham Fair
Be sure an call at The Hole in the Waa'
For there you get whiskey for nowt
An' brandy for nothing at aa'

The Castle Inn was also a great place for food and drink, being a busy post house where the horses were changed on the main Newcastle to Edinburgh route. Here Pickwickian characters would demand vast pies and ale to fortify them on their gruelling journey. Sunday was always a day of rest and it was the pleasant tradition that the landlord would treat any guests to supper if they would buy a drink to toast the health of their host. A civilised custom which sadly died out with the stage coach.

Until the early 1800's Whittingham held a mammoth fair on St Bartholomew, the villages patron saint's day. There were stalls of cow cheese from the Breamish, ale and gingerbread as well as boxing booths, musicians and droves of sheep and cattle. The Whittingham Games continue the tradition with the ever popular Cumberland wrestling, beer tent and the W.I's cakes and biscuits.

Whittingham Buttons

12 ozs margarine	*6 ozs icing sugar*
12 ozs pl. flour	*4 ozs custard powder*

Cream margarine and icing sugar. Add flour and custard powder and mix till stiff and smooth. Roll onto small balls and flatten down with the back of a fork. Bake in a moderate oven until pale, golden brown.

Mrs Dunn's Soft Gingerbread

8 fl.ozs milk	*4 ozs lard or marg.*
8 ozs pl flour	*$^1/_2$ tspn bicarb*
4 ozs dark treacle	*2 tspns ginger*
4 ozs golden syrup	*2 tspns mixed spice*
4 ozs brown sugar	*1 egg*

Warm milk, treacle and fat until melted. Mix dry ingredients. Beat egg and mix all together. Pour into a lined, greased tin. Cook Mark 3 for 11/4 hours

Taking the road to Callaly we pass what was Dixon's the Grocers, with its original sign. It is now run by Allie Warenford and Peter Stone who are reviving the tradition for local cheeses, eggs, preserves and vegetables when ever they are available as well as an amazing range of tea, coffee, and wines.

Approaching Callaly castle there is a sign warning that a deer might land on the bonnet of your car. The walled parkland round the castle was at one time inhabited by them, possibly the pretty spotted Fallows which now are to be found only in the parks at Alnwick and Chillingham. Nowadays it is the smaller roe deer which roam the woods in large numbers. Routine culling takes place as the numbers rise and tree damage occurs.

Venison is growing in popularity and is widely available throughout the county direct from the big estates, game dealers or butchers. It was traditionally eaten only by the nobility and game laws were so strict that poaching was often a hanging offence. Boiled venison was often eaten with frumenty. "Fat venison with frumentry-it is a gay pleasure "wrote a local connosieur.

Frumenty to be eaten with venison or porpoise

10 ozs wheat or barley   *2 well beaten egg yolks*

2 pts of creamy milk   *pinch of saffron*

$1^1/_2$ *pt water*

Wash the grain and put in a covered pan with the water. Cook slowly until it is gelatinous. It will keep up to three days in this state. Add milk and boil until it is very thick. It can be coloured by adding the egg yolks and saffron.

The best joints are the saddle and the haunch which should be marinated before roasting. The tougher parts can be cooked slowly in wine and make terrific casseroles. Even the offal or umbles used to be eaten hences the phrase, "eating humble pie" meaning to take a lowly position.

Umble Pie

Take the umbles of a deer, boil until tender and when cold, mince small with an equal quantity of beef suet and six large apples, half a pound of currants and as much sugar. Add to them as much salt, nutmeg and pepper as your palate will relish. Mix all together and bake with a thick crust. Pour into your pie a pint of canary the juice of two Seville oranges and one lemon and serve hot.

The road leading into the hamlet of Callaly is lined with magnificent beech trees which give shade and shelter to a host of wild animals, especially the red squirrels which flourish on the beech mast. One Elizabethan gourmet wrote of this dear creature "Their hinder parts are indifferent good when they are young, fried with parsley and butter."

The Lorbottle estate today consists of a manor house tucked away in the trees, now the country retreat of a famous London fashion designer, and a few cottages and farmhouses. The old "towre" was devastated by the Scots in 1532 and again in 1549 when

Mark Ker rode on and Mark Ker rode on,
But never a hoof or horn saw he
Till he came to the ford of Lorbottle Burn
Where a dainty drove lay on the lea

In 1648 the efficient Roundheads captured yet another party of sleepy Cavaliers, taking "sixty horse and sixty men, all in bed." Cavaliers were always kind to their animals!

Lorbottle is best known for a strange group of inhabitants called the Lorbottle "Cubs", "Kebs" or "Coves", famous for their greed and enormous eating capacity which gave rise to the verse.

Yor as bad as the Kebs of Lorbottle
Ye'll eat nineteen penny loaves to a pint
of yeal and cry for more stuffing.

51

These intellectually challenged folk were credited with strange failings, including not being able to sort out their own limbs on rising from the table and consequently falling over. When the moon rose behind Lough Crag, believing it to be a massive red cheese, they set out with ropes to haul it down and eat it.

Rooks and pigeons abound in this area and on the crowstep gable of an ancient building at Cartington a carved stone pigeon roosts, battered by the wind and rain. Whether it was a decoy, a decoration or more likely a dovecote, is hard to say. Rooks and pigeons were popular fare for the poor. Rooks are now protected and can only be shot by license at certain times of the year.

Rook Pie

(The recipe says to pluck the birds, but, as with pheasants, it is much easier to skin them.) Keep only the legs and breasts. Put in a pan with cold water and a big bunch of majoram, sage and thyme and an onion. Cook slowly until all the meat comes off the bone. Layer the meat in a pie dish, with rings of hard boiled eggs. Heat enough of the liquor to cover and dissolve 1/2oz of gelatine to each pint and pour over the meat. Cover with rich shortcrust or raised pie pastry and cook until brown. Leave overnight to cool then serve with a fresh green salad.

Cartington Castle dates back to the 1360's and was home to a succession of powerful knights. In 1515 Queen Margaret of Scotland stayed here for four days with the heiress of Cartington, Lady Ann Redcliff. Having just given birth to a daughter at Harbottle, she had to be carried on a litter and was no doubt grateful for a few days of generous hospitality before continuing her long and dangerous journey south.

Medieval entertaining was always lavish. A typical meal for an honoured guest might consist of a "sallet" of roast beef, venison baked in pastry, chickens or possibly, a whole roasted swan a cured swanskin being kept to put over the cooked bird. Directions for cooking are rather gruesome.

52

Kutte a Swan in the rove of the mouthe toward the brayne enlonge, and lete him blede and kepe the blode for chawdewyn, oe elles knytte a knot on his nek, and so late his nekee breke; then scald him. Drawe him and rost him even as thou doest goce.

After all this the flesh was always like old boots. No wonder medieval teeth didn't last very long.

Cartington Castle has been put on the map more recently by the present owners, the Murray family who produce a range of "Cheviot Castle" spring water bearing a picture of Cartington Castle on the label. Until Victorian times water was considered only fit for the poor and animals. With the adulteration of many of our modern water supplies with an increasing number of dubious chemicals, the market for bottled water is enormous.

Cartington Castle

Dropping down into the valley, the village of Snitter is on our right. The Half Moon Inn, now a private house, was the social centre where cockfighting and cardplaying were the activities and legs of mutton the stakes.

It was also one of many taverns where a traditional "Braxy Supper" was held to celebrate the end of winter. This exotic sounding affair was in fact a companionable way to get rid of lamb which had succumbed to a disease called Braxy. The mainstay of the dinner was a thick broth made from the aforesaid sheep and vegetables.

A good time was had by all and no one developed Braxy. A chairman and committee were elected to run the affair and it continued at Snitter until 1929 when the pub was sold. The Coquetvale Hotel in Rothbury revived this custom recently with mutton minus the Braxy which is a thing of the past due to modern vaccination of sheep.

Turning left at The Cross Keys in Thropton, we finish our hard days food trailing with the reward of dinner at the Corn Road Restaurant. This attractive stone house in Bridge Street dates back to the 1600's and as its name suggests was on the busy ancient road which brought corn from Hexhamshire and all point west to the port of Alnmouth, where it was exported, free of tax.

Graham Hodgson and his partner Pam have developed their business very carefully with the traditions and history of the village in mind. They aim to provide a relaxed and cost atmosphere for a few, with an interesting and varied menu made from the best quality local produce, freshly bought and cooked. The emphasis is on taste and colour.

Such a civilised attitude to food does pay, as the restaurant not only appeals to visitors who want to try Northumbrian fare, but ensures that local people come here regularly all year round, knowing that they will enjoy an excellent and unhurried meal in pleasant surroundings.

Corn Road

Trail Three
Roman Road
Herbs
and
Spices

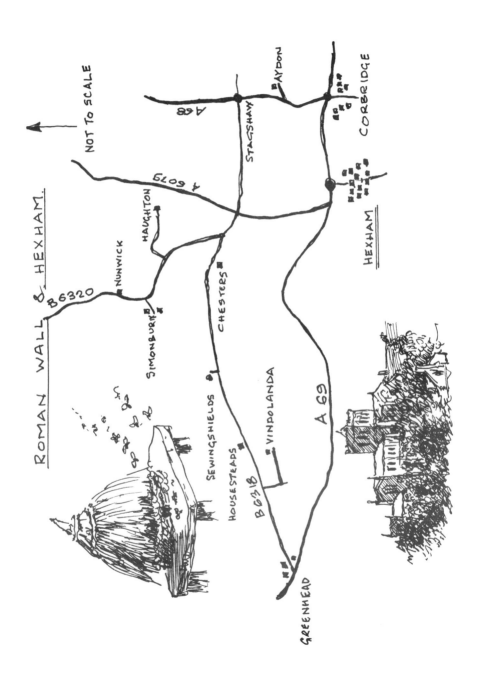

Roman Road
Herbs and Spices

This trail has a decidedly Roman flavour. As well as their great military and building skills, the Romans brought sophistication and variety in the form of new herbs and spices to liven up the boring British "meat and two veg."

Our tour starts in the market town of Hexham. According to some historians this was once a Roman station. It is perhaps more likely that several important Roman civilians had villas here, conveniently placed away from the main rabble of soldiery living in Corbridge.

Despite Miss Mary Mitford's scathing remarks made in 1806 that "she had dined at a very wretched inn" and confessed that Hexham was a "shocking gloomy place" it is packed with wonderful buildings reflecting its Roman, Saxon, Medieval and Victorian past.

Dominating the Town is the Abbey. Begun by St Wilfred in 674, it was built in the impressive Roman style. Despite the Reformation and Border raids it remains a treasure house of exciting features. Prior Leschman's Chantry filled with carvings, including a fox, dressed as a monk and reading a sermon and a monkey feasting on buns which are full of the humour and humanity of its carver.

Market Place

Adjoining the Abbey is the Market Place which has been a major centre for food traders since the thirteenth century. In 1239, as now, there was a weekly market. In 1319 two large fairs lasting five or six days were initiated. By 1522 the local "mafia" had moved in and crime was rife. Neither "poor men, gentlemen and their goody's" (A lovely if sexist term for "the wife") were safe from cutpurses and vagabonds.

By the early 1800's shopping had become more civilised and the market was famous for high quality cheap meat, poultry, butter and eggs. Fish was scarce because the carriage from east or west coast was too expensive. Few vegetables were sold as everyone grew their own and sent any surplus to the Newcastle Market.

Gardener's Boiled Salad

This goes very well with home cooked ham or gammon

Boiled onions, beetroot, cauli-
flower or broccoli heads,
celery, french beans
2 ozs currants soaked for $^1/_2$ an
hour in cold water

1 crisp lettuce
1 tspn chopped herbs
A good oil and vinegar dressing

Very lightly cook a small quantity of all the vegetables separately in a little well salted water. Drain and cool. Cut into neat pieces. Arrange lettuce in a large flat dish and pour over a little dressing. Pile all the vegetables on it, keeping the beetroot separate. Pour over rest of dressing. Drain currants and sprinkle over with parsley and mixed herbs.

Grain was brought to Hexham in large quantities. Two breweries run by Messers Elstob and Anderson operated in the town and a Mr Dixon ran the Tyne corn mills. Three ancient mills existed for all the local farmers and bakers who had to provide their own flour sacks and horse transport.

Thirty two inns supported the brewers. There was a preponderance of Bulls for some reason. The Royal Hotel of today was once The Low Grey Bull. Whether this referred to the stature of the animal or the quality of the clients is not clear. This was the starting point of the "British Queen" coach which made its four hour journey to Newcastle every morning, keeping commuters to a minimum.

Further up the street was The High Grey Bull and in the Market Place, the Black Bull was the scene of a curious and bitter culinary fracas.

This "Upstairs, Downstairs" saga began in 1747 with the publication of "The Art of Cookery made Plain and Easy, which far Exceeds anything of the kind yet Published By a Lady." This provocative title was the work of Mrs Hannah

Glasse, a member of the well connected Allgood family's she had run away at the age of sixteen with a poor but no doubt handsome soldier. Perhaps to raise a little revenue she decided to write her book. Life is ironic as a first edition of her work can fetch £6000 among todays collectors.

This delightful book not only included advice on Hog's puddings, soups and pretty little dishes for a Great Table, but a "cure for the bite of a mad dog; how a Captain should set his table on board ship and a "receipt to keep clear from Buggs."

Mrs Glasse was obviously an authority on everything under the sun and as such a major irritation. Mrs Anne Cook, the landlady of the Black Bull certainly thought so. Calling herself a "Teacher of the True Art of Cookery". Anne proceeded to pull Hannah's methods apart;

If genealogy was understood
Its all a Farce, her Title is not good.
Can seed of Noble Blood or renown'd Squire
Teach drudges to clean spits or build up Fires?

A feud developed. Lancelot Allgood, Hannah's brother who used to stay at the Bull during the Assizes, swore that while he could forgive the husband he would be "the destruction of the Bitch, his wife."

The Cooks were forced to move to The Black Bull in Morpeth, only to be further hounded and finally made bankrupt. The indomitable Mrs Glasse continued to write and her recipe books are still revered by many English cooks.

Mrs Glasse's Whipped Syllabub 1769

$^1/_2$ bottle claret	juice or 2 oranges
3 ozs caster sugar	grated peel of 1 orange & 1
1 pt thick cream	lemon
$^1/_2$ pt sherry	$^1/_2$ lb caster sugar

Mix all but the claret and 3ozs of castor sugar together in a wide bowl. Beat well and skim off the froth as it rises, placing it in a sieve to drain. Fill some small glasses with the sweetened claret, pile the drained froth on these and serve. (Mrs G suggests the liquid which remains in the bowl can be set with a calves foot to make a jelly).

Hexham in Victorian times reflected the typical English class system of the aspiring middle and upper eschelons and the very poor. One report speaks of a select society in the town where card parties, music and dancing, elegant conversation, going to the races and attending the "commodious little theatre" was accompanied by equally delicate fare.

Victorian Simple Sponge

3 eggs

3ozs flour

3ozs sugar

Break the eggs into a large bowl. Add the sieved sugar and whisk until the mixture is thick and creamy. Add the sieved flour and fold in with a whisk. Pour into a well greased 8" tin. Bake at 375F for 10mins then reduce to 350F for 15 - 20 mins. Turn out onto wire tray and eat as soon as it is cool.

At the other end of the scale was the Poor House in Priestpopple. This cost the parish 2s 6d for each inmate paid to the "Master". The provisions here were much more basic and traditional. On Sundays and Thursdays there was boiled beef, broth, pease pudding and vegetables. Tuesdays and Fridays were "Collop" days. Collops were generally slices of salt bacon, fried. Collop Monday, just before Lent was one of the last days that meat could be eaten before the Easter Fast.

This was good fare compared to the many times when harvests were bad and food scarce. Then a thin gruel of flour the Hexham Poorhouse and the Master "recommended to the nice stomached lady of quality, an occasional peep into a poor house." For her benefit or that of the inmates is not clear.

Hexham Collops

1 lb minced beef or chopped ba-
con
1 large onion
1 tbspn oatmeal

1oz dripping
8 fl ozs water
salt and pepper

Brown the meat and chopped onion in the dripping. Season well. Add oatmeal and water. Cover and simmer for 30 minutes. Can be served with a poached egg.

Modern Hexam is full of good food. If fish was rare in the eighteenth century, Ridley's Fish and Game Shop on Battle Hill is more than making up for it. Here David and Carolyn Ridley have spent the last two and a half years maintaining and extending the service provided by the Murray family for two generations.

The traditional window display of fresh white fish from Amble, Wild salmon, trout, Craster kippers and Lindisfarne oysters all packed in ice is a work of art. More exotic produce from all over the world is also available but local produce is very important to the Ridley's.

Fresh game, venison, rabbit, (ferreted not shot, which saves a trip to the dentist) hare, pheasants are all local and the plump free range chickens are bought from the Cumberland border.

David's Chicken And Leek Pie

1 medium roasting chicken or 2	8-10 fresh sage leaves
boiling fowl	a little oil and butter
2 large leeks	4 ozs plain flour
2 large carrots	$^1/_2$ pt milk
1 onion	Ground black pepper
4 bay leaves	pastry

Poach chicken in water with herbs and pepper. Boiling fowl will take 2 $^1/_2$ hours, the chicken approximately 1 $^1/_2$ hours. When ready allow to cool in stock. Meanwhile make pastry. Sweat off chopped onion in oil and butter. Add flour and work in with a spoon, gradually add milk and cook. Add some stock stirring all the time until you have a smooth not too thick sauce. Add chopped carrots and cook for 5 minutes. Add chopped rings of leek and simmer for further 5 minutes. Remove meat from chickens and arrange neatly in a pie dish. add the sauce. Roll out pastry to 1/8" and egg wash sides of dish. Lay pastry and decorate. Bake at Gas 4 for 25-30 minutes.

David also buys in special Cumbrian/Northumbrian sausage from Billy Bell at Haltwhistle and haggis is made to a recipe from the Royal Balmoral Hotel at Ballater. David who was previously a chef at Langley Castle and Carolyn who is a professional caterer, have developed an excellent range of homemade pies and crumbles which are sold fresh in the shop.

Customers can choose from chicken and leek Hot Pot, Cottage Pie, Fishermans Pie topped with potato or breadcrumbs and fruit pies and crumbles. There are also excellent fresh salmon and dill fish cakes, game pies and stuffing made with fresh herbs from Mill Cottage Allenheads

Ridley's Smoked and Fresh Salmon Roulade

4ozs Robson's of Craster's sliced smoked salmon

8ozs skinless, boneless wild fresh salmon

$^1/_4$ pt Hellmans mayonnaise

3 ozs fromage frais

$^1/_4$ pt whipping cream

4 large eggs, separated

salt and pepper

fresh chopped dill, keep stalks

2 bay leaves

$^1/_2$ tspn Worcester sauce

1tstspn brandy

Bring fresh salmon to boil in a little water with bay leaves and dill stalks. Simmer for one minute. Take off heat and allow to cool in stock then drain. Grease and line with greaseproof paper a 15"" swiss roll tin. Whip cream until fairly stiff. Separate eggs and add yolk to cream. Gently fold in fromage frais plus seasoning and half the chopped dill. Whisk egg whites till peaked and fold them very gently into mixture. Spoon into lined tin and bake at Gas mark four for ten to fifteen minutes until firm and golden. Leave to cool. Mix smoked and fresh salmon, add remainder of chopped dill and mayonnaise and mix. Add Worcester sauce and brandy. Lay out a sheet of greaseproof paper and turn out the sponge, top side down. Carefully peel off original paper. Spread salmon mix carefully onto sponge. Taking the top of the greaseproof paper, roll it towards you into a swiss roll. Leave in paper and chill for one hour before serving.

For meat, Edward Robson's at 3, Cattlemarket, is the place to go in this family business started by the present owner Clive's great grandfather, properly hung, well flavoured meat has always been offered. The shop is uncluttered by burgers, kebabs and such trivia. This is a place for the serious meat eater where the excellent joints of locally reared beef and lamb are all that matters. Clive's only concession to "convenience" food is his own pork and beef sausage. It is understandable that Clive regrets the decline in popularity of the Sunday roast and the excellent slower cooking cuts in favour of the mass mince market used for lasagne, chilli and other foreign fare.

In Sarah Hedley's delicatessen with the unlikely Northumbrian name of "C'est Cheese" there is a host of produce from far afield, but more importantly local fare is not neglected. Mark Robertson's sheep, goat and cow cheeses from his Elsdon Dairy are stocked and Caroline Dickinson's wonderful range of homemade soups. These include Northumbrian Neep and Nip, watercress and mushroom, carrot and orange, leek and potato and farmhouse tomato. Caroline is a Cordon Bleu cook and farmer's wife from Brockbushes farm, near Stocksfield. Part of the farm is turned over to large scale fruit and vegetable production, which is sold direct to the public and allows Caroline a choice of completely fresh ingredients for her soups.

Hexham Market which still takes place every Tuesday is an excellent place to buy good quality, extremely cheap fruit and vegetables. There are also fresh eggs from Giles Dowdell but Mrs Winne Rowell, and Miss Molly Gallon, who run the Abbey Gift Shop, can remember when all the farmer's wives from the shire brought their butter, eggs and baking to sell in town while their husbands went to the mart.

Corbridge is our next port of call, which because of its ideal situation next to woods, moors and the River Tyne has always had free access to food from the wild. Because of this it is one of the most ancient settlements in the country. Neolithic, Bronze and Iron age remains have been found here and for the same reasons the Romans chose to build a major settlement here on the site of a previous British homestead.

Corstopitum, as it was called in Roman times, was a small metropolis of butchers bakers, granaries and workshops, employing many of the different races which made up the Roman Empire. It is thought that a large number of people of oriental extraction were also based here. Built at the junction of two major Roman Roads, Dere Street and Stanegate it was also a centre for trade.

A survey of animal bones and teeth found on the site suggest that beef in large quantities was eaten by most of the population. This was followed by mutton, lamb, horse and pork. The Romans were responsible for introducing new and more efficient farming practices to this country. Enclosing pigs and poultry and feeding them on grain being one. The following recipe which uses pork, leeks, herbs and spices is of Roman origin.

Roman Pork And Leeks.

2 lbs of pork chops cut up	*2 tbspns spns parsley*
1 lb cooking apples	*1 tbspn spn mint*
1 pt stock	*wine vinegar*
1 lb leeks	*1 tspn salt*
6 peppercorns	*1 tspn honey*
1 tbspn spn coriander	*butter for frying*

Heat butter, fry meat for five minutes. Add stock, chopped leeks, parsley and salt. Stew for ten minutes. Add chopped apples, grind pepper and add with coriander and mint, a few drops of wine vinegar and honey. Put in a stew pan and cook gently until tender.

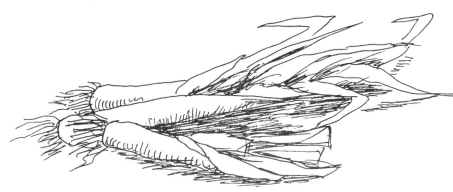

Bread was an important part of the Roman soldier's ration and he was allowed beef and 3lbs of bread or cereal a day. The wealthy Roman citizens ate only white, refined bread, often made whiter by the addition of chalk. The military bread was the ultimate in the "nowt taken owt" league, being very brown and gritty and full of husks and bran. Barley bannocks and oat hearthcakes were also common fare. Wheaton loaves were often broken into large pieces, soaked in milk, fried in oil and eaten covered in honey.

Honey was much favoured in Roman cooking, being used to sweeten just about everything and also as a preservative for meat and fruit. In Northumberland large birds like herons were cooked in honey. This recipe substitutes turkey as herons are in short supply.

Turkey In Honey

1 lb medium thick honey for a 15-20 lb bird

$^1/_2$ lb butter

Melt butter and honey and stir until mixed. Place Turkey in a baking tray and cover with honey mixture. Leave for an hour, basting frequently. Roast at 400F for thirty minutes til an almost black crust forms. Baste with juices. Reduce to 350F cook for thirty minutes. Cover with foil and cook as usual. Remove foil 15 minutes before cooking completed. Honey seals in the flavour and juices making the meat white and tender and the skin sweet and crunchy.

Corbridge continued to flourish until the fourteenth century when two hundred years of plague, first the disease and then the Scots, decimated the area. In Saxon times it was a significant town, possibly a royal seat when Bamburgh declined. St. Andrew's church which was dedicated in 786 is of interest for many reasons, but especially for the west tower which is built from Roman Stones. The massive triumphal arch to the east of the porch is believed to have been moved intact from a nearby Roman site.

The churchyard is equally notable. On the south side is a superb three storied pele tower completed in the Thirteen Hundreds. To the west is the King's Oven where the community brought all their bread and probably meat to be baked.

Pele Tower

66

The medieval market place with its stone cross set on a Roman altar was the scene of constant activity. A weekly market served a large rural area and the narrow streets were filled with visitors to the bread and wine stalls and bringing goods to barter. Penalties for theft at such events were dire and the unfortunately named Thomas Onion and his mother, Catalina, occupants of an old mill, were sentenced to death for stealing meat from Sir Richard de Hethington.

By eighteen thirty, Corbridge was at a very low point in its history and it was reported as being a filthy, run down place with an unhappy, malnourished population. Such is not the case today and Corbridge is once again a flourishing and affluent village, popular with Northumbrians and visitors. As well as its peaceful atmosphere and beautifully preserved buildings, it also has a tempting selection of unusual shops catering especially for those interested in fashion and food.

As this is a tasty trail we must concentrate on the food and a good place to start is in the Corbridge Larder, situated in Heron House on Hill Street. Once through the seventeenth century doorway there are shelves piled high with treats. From North Acomb Farm near Hexham comes home cured bacon, sausages, butter and cream. There is cheese from Redesdale, Northumbrian Honey from Burswell Cottage, Hexham and free range eggs from Five Dykes Farm, Steel.

Particularly attractive are the large selection of jewel coloured jellies, marmalades and chutneys made by the indefatigable Mrs Clarke from Loughbrow House, Hexham. She produces all these without any preservatives, using only apple juice to help with the setting and all the ingredients come from her own large garden and orchard.

In the 'Larder' there are Rhubarb and ginger jam and peach and almond conserve. The crystal clear jellies include Apple with Rosemary, Rowan or Sweet Geranium, Gooseberry and Elderflower, Redcurrant and Marjoram, Crabapple and Bramble. The Marmalades, Threefruit, Grapefruit and Seville are full of fruit and the chutneys, Green tomato, Damson, Beetroot, Rhubarb and Horseradish are spicey and fragrant. All these are made to Mrs Clarke's own traditional recipes and refined during many years over a hot stove.

Blackberry And Sloe Jelly

Northumbrian hedgerows in the Autumn are the perfect place to find the ingredients for this.

4 lbs blackberries

1 lb sloes

Sugar prick sloes with a needle, put in a pan with the blackberries. Cover with water, simmer until tender. Strain through a jelly bag and measure liquid. Add one pound of sugar to each pint of juice. Heat juice gently until sugar has dissolved then boil hard until setting point is reached. Remove any surface scum. Pour into warm jars. This dark ruby red jelly with a hint of tartness is marvellous with meat.

Just across the road is J.A. Hall's family butcher, the home of a prizewinning Cumberland sausage with sage. All the beef and lamb here is locally reared and slaughtered and home cured bacon comes from Philip L Leadbetter at Lemmington.

Round the corner on Middle Street, there are yet more food finds. Here in the Corbridge Seafood shop Robert Latimer is building up an excellent business. Robert, who has gained his experience on Scottish Fish Farms is now filling his shop with the best local fish, shellfish, wild game, poultry and fresh eggs.

Good places to buy cooking equipment are few and far between, so it is a bonus to find J.F. Walton and Sons Aladdin's cave just at the other side of the street, full of bain maries and madelaine tins and exciting gadgets to core apples and cut pastry.

On the same side at the end of Middle Street is Nichol and Laidlaw's Baker's shop "manned" by Heather Curry. This is an offshoot of their main branch in Hexham which also has a cosy tea and coffee shop. A longstanding family business, their breads have evocative names like the oatie bobble and oatie bloomer, both of which sound like obscure items of Victorian clothing. There is a square oatie, a dark rye and wholemeal loaf and the flat Northumbrian Stottie. Specialities are Hexham shortbread and Old Mill flour which is ground at Wark, several miles up the river.

Flour was always a vital commodity for the poor. Around Corbridge in the eighteen hundreds a heavy harvest was important to the farmer and his men. In a good year a Harvest Supper of beef and beer was laid on by the Master for all to enjoy. After this the workers or their wives could gather the gleanings which would be kept through the winter to make bread or crowdie.

Boiled Beef In Beer

This local recipe was used for harvest and haymaking suppers. The meaner farmers sometimes used a tough old or sick animal that wouldn't make it through the autumn.

1 quart light ale to every 4lb	*Turmeric,*
beef	*12 peppercorns,*
4-12 lbs lean beef, well tied	*Salt*
2-4 lbs onions	*$^1/_4$ pt wine vinegar*
Large bundle sweet herbs	*4 ozs dark treacle to every 4 lbs*
3 cloves	*meat*
Mace,	

Pile the onions on top of the beef and marinate overnight in all the ingredients except the ale. Put meat, onions and marianade in a very large pan and cover well with the beer. Simmer very gently for about 3 hours until tender.

Local records of eighteen twenty nine show that many farmworkers didn't receive wages but were allowed produce from the farm and a free cottage. A typical agreement was for the worker to keep a pig and a cow, for which they were given grazing, one ton of hay and tenloads of turnips. They also had access to one hundred yards of potato drill and twenty four pounds of wool to spin for clothing. A ration of corn would be made into meal for crowdie and oatcakes and a small income made by selling surplus milk, butter and pork.

Finding a good master and a permanent job was the sole aim of may agricultural workers. All too often when May Day came they found themselves unemployed and on the move again, with a cartload of children and furniture. If it was simply a case of moving from one farm to another the well prepared mother would make two or three 'Flittin Dumplins' in advance. These would be hung up in calico bags, ready for the journey to the new home, when they could be quickly heated up to provide a hot and filling first meal until they got properly settled.

Flittin Dumplin

2 large cups plain flour

1 tspn bicarbonate of soda

1 cup chopped walnuts

12 ozs chopped dates or other fruit

$^3/_4$ large cup golden syrup

$^1/_2$ tspn salt

1 large cup of milk

Mix all dry ingredients together. Warm the milk and add syrup and bicarbonate. Make well in centre of flour and pour in liquid. Mix well and pour into a greased tin or pudding bain, cover with greaseproof paper and steam for approx. three hours.

70

Flittin Day

The village inn was an important social institution for rich and poor through centuries and Corbridge still has several old taverns. The Wheatsheaf, once thatched, has a Roman stone figure of Ceres, the goddess of harvest and fertility, in the stable yard. The Angel on Main Street, dates back to Tudor times. Above the front street door is a sundial dated 1726 and carved with the initials E.W.A. for Edward and Anne Winship. As "The Head Inn" in 1752, it was the post house for the weekly mail coach. It is now a comfortable hotel with a restaurant that serves some of the best locally produced food in the county. The Chef, Richard Simm, and Proprietor, Mandy McIntosh Reid have searched for the best Northumbrian ingredients to create some really interesting dishes which deserve to become part of local tradition.

For example Smoked Craster pheasant is enhanced with toasted hazelnuts and caramelised plums. A steamed fillet of local salmon is cooked with a vermouth sauce and raw or cooked Lindisfarne oysters. There are various cuts of Cheviot and Tynedale lamb, sauteed pigeons wrapped in bacon and Boulmer crabmeat tartlet.

It is a pleasure to find a chef who appreciates the quality and variety of Northumbrian raw ingredients and has the confidence to make them the focal point of his menu. This area is awash with Chinese, Indian and Italian restaurants, all excellent in their way. But surely what visitors particularly want and what restauranteurs should be proud to offer, is the authentic local cuisine.

In France, each region glories in its specialities. This not only provides pleasure for the tourist but is a help to the local economy. Britain on the other hand is in great danger of losing what is best in pursuit of a quick turn over and international blandness. Richard Simm and a few others have the right outlook and are putting Northumberland on the map as a centre of culinary excellence.

When Aydon Castle was built in 1250, by Peter de Vallibus, using local produce was the only option. All the meat, vegetables, fruit and grain would be produced on the estate.

This beautifully compact fortified manor was passed to Robert de Raymes in 1296 Teetering on the very edge of the deep ravine of the Cor Burn, it is H shaped with towers at each corner. The massive outerwall has arrow slits and there are three courtyards making it virtually impregnable.

Inside,the vast sixteenth century fireplace and the first story Great Hall conjure up the scale of ceremony and entertainment practised in the fourteenth century.

One person who makes this past come vividly alive is Lesley Hayman who, dressed as the gracious Lady Joan de Raymes, welcomes groups of schoolchildren, also dressed in medieval costume to her "Stately home." As well as attempting calligraphy and candle making, the children have to prepare their own medieval meal. This involves chopping herbs and vegetables for the pottage, arranging a "sallat" and cheese and putting chicken joints into muslin bags to be cooked, along with the soup, in a large cauldron over an open fire.

The meal is served in the Great Hall by some of the children to their classmates, all learning at first hand and with much enjoyment, the complicated rituals and social structures associated with a noble family.

Medieval mealtimes reinforced the hierarchy of class and involved everyone in the household in what seems a marvellous exercise in job creation. Even on non festive occasions, rituals were observed. The lord and lady ate at table "above the salt" which, as a precious commodity, was kept in a decorative silver cellar. The table was prepared by the sewers, warm herb filled water was presented by the ewerers, the butler and the cellarar decanted the wine and ale and the cupbearer presented it to the Lord in his own special cup.

The panter in the "panterie", hence our word pantry, selected the best bread. The expression "upper crust" is derived from this practice where the loaf was cut horizontally and the master given the tastiest upper portion.

Plates were very rare and food was usually served on thick slices of bread called trenchers. The nobleman might have a stack of these at each meal, one for the various courses. The ordinary man only had one. At the end of the meal these were collected in the alms dish by the almoner and given to the poor.

73

Grape Stuffed Boiled Chicken

It was quite comman for more exotic fruits to be grown in sheltered court-yards. This meal would be eaten on a flesh-day.

2 small chickens, approx
$2^1/_2$ lbs each
8 ozs green grapes
minced parsley and fresh sage
leaves to coat grapes

4 garlic cloves
salt and ground black pepper
$1^1/_2$ pts good chicken stock
powder-douce*

Prepare birds for boiling. Halve and seed grapes or use seedless variety. Coat grapes thickly with herbs. Crush garlic, add to grapes, season well and stuff the birds. truss to enclose stuffing. Place birds on a thick cloth in a stewpan. Add enough stock to come 3/4 way up their sides. Bring slowly to boil, lower heat and simmer for about 45 minutes. Place on a warm dish and sprinkle with powder-douce. *Powder-douce was widely used for flavouring and consisted of $^1/_2$ tspn each of cinnamon, nutmeg and ground black pepper and 1tspn white sugar.

Returning to the A68 and travelling north, the road passes a large area of rough scrubland on the right. This was once the site of Stagshaw Fair, one of the oldest and largest in the country. It was last held in the 1930's and was possibly begun in Roman times. Because of its position near so many major roads, including the ancient drove roads from Scotland it attracted people and cattle and sheep from all over the Borders. Sometimes there were up to 100,00 sheep, plus cattle,horses and pigs. It was a spectacle not to be missed. Wombell's wonderful menagerie with lions was an added attraction in the 1830's.

Everything was sold here, especially food and drink. there were stalls filled with gingerbread, oranges, cherries, bread and cakes and spices from London. The farmers bought tools and saddlery, while their wives lingered at the jewellery stall or tried on a pair of famous "Hexham tans"gloves. There was something for everyone, from bee skeps to books.

On the left side of the road is the early eighteenth century Stagshaw House, one time home of a Mr Ridley, who , on returning from Australia, invented a new reaping machine, a prototype of the combine harvester which separated the heads from the stalks and funnelled the grain into sacks. The stubble could then be burnt to fertilize the field.

Turning left at Stagshaw roundabout the road passes the chapel of St Oswald which was rebuilt in 1737. King Oswald of Northumbria raised his standard here at the battle of Hefenfelt, or Heavenfield as it is now called, in AD 65.

Oswald's brother Eanfrith had been traitorously killed by the aptly named Cadwallader. Greatly outnumbered, the Christian king prayed for victory and was rewarded. Cadwallader fled off down Watling Street, only to be caught and killed at Rowley Burn. Heavenfield has since been thought of as a place with great powers of healing.

Dropping down we cross the elegant five arched bridge over the Tyne at Chollerford. It was erected in 1755 after the original of 1333 was destroyed in a flood. The bridge was vital to trade as the nearby ford was often too dangerous to cross. A Roman bridge upstream carried the line of Hadrians Wall across the river to the fort at Chesters.

What is now the "George Hotel" was known as the "New Inn" in the early eighteenth century. In 1776 an unfortunate stork who made a flying visit to the tavern, was shot and his skin nailed to the wall in the bar; an early and rather macabre tourist attraction.

A little further downstream below the pretty village of Humshaugh is Haughton Castle. In Henry VIII's reign the owner, Sir Thomas Swinburne captured a notorious mosstrooper called Archie Armstrong and threw him in a dungeon before galloping off to an important meeting in York with Cardinal Wolsey.

On the fourth day, as he sighted York, Sir Thomas remembered that he had left no instructions to feed or water poor Archie. He must have been an extremely kind man, instead of saying good riddance, he turned his confused horse and dashed back north. The unhappy animal dropped dead in Durham and mounted on another, good Sir Thomas flew back to Haughton. Too late. The undiscovered Archie was dead, starved to death, having tried to eat the flesh from his own arms to survive.

Until a few years ago a ferry was pulled across the North Tyne from Haughton to Barrasford by an overhead rope and pulley. What makes this so amazing is that it was initiated over eight hundred years ago in 1189 by Runulph de Halvton and William de Swinburne who agreed to share the running costs.

The Ferry at Haughton, 1890's

Returning to the B631 we are back on the Roman Wall. On the left is the major fort at Chesters. Here are the remains of the finest military bath house in Britain and two enormous granaries to cater for the needs of the 512 cavalrymen and their horses who were stationed here.

There was probably a civil settlement attached to the six acre military site to grow and prepare food for the troops. Cavalry regiments being more "upmarket" than the regular foot soldier, the quality of their food and drink was probably equally so.

Large quantities of shellfish remains have been found all along the Wall, indicating that the practise of transporting mussels, cockles, whelks and oysters in tanks of sea water to keep them fresh was carried out here.

This recipe for lentil soup with mussels was special to this area, almost equidistant between the east and west coast. It is typical of the Romans use of herbs, spices and honey to flavour their food.

Lentil and Mussel Soup

1 cup lentils	*1 tspn rue*
2 pts water	*1 tbspn vinegar*
2 bay leaves	*1 tspn honey*
$^1/_2$ tspn peppercorns	*1$^1/_2$ tspns salt*
$^1/_2$ tspn cumin seeds	*mint*
$^1/_2$ tspn coriander seeds	*1$^1/_2$ cups boiled mussels*

Wash lentils, place in pan with water. Cook on gentle heat until soft. Pound seeds with herbs. Moisten with vinegar. Add honey and salt and mussels. Cook for a further 15 minutes. Add rest of vinegar and serve.

Many of the recipes use liquamen which was a very salty concoction of mullet, sprats, anchovies and fish entrails which were salted and left in the sun. The resulting juice was used rather as we might use Worcester sauce. Oysters, another Roman favourite, were stewed in liquamen, vinegar, oil, honey and wine with pepper, lovage and the yolk of an egg.

Goats were a common source of food and were kept in large herds along the Wall where there was plenty rough grazing for them. Wild thistle juice was used to coagulate the milk for cheesemaking. it was then drained in wicker baskets and salted, smoked or mixed with herbs. Soldiers carried curd cheese with them on their marches as well as bacon fat, corn, sour wine and bread. Mustard was another Roman introduction. They used it with sausage, boiled boar and stuffed udder, usually from a sow, sometimes from a cow, the latter remained popular until the middle ages.

The Roman introduction and use of so many new herbs and spices is recreated half a mile from Chesters in the glorious walled garden that is now Hexham Herbs, one of the best collections of unusual culinary plants in the country.

This was originally the gardens for the country house built by John Errington in 1771 and extended by John Dobson in 1832. It has been turned into a plantsman's paradise by Susie White. Hardy, healthy specimens of nearly every culinary herb can be bought here. The Roman garden which was established in 1988 is of particular interest on our trail.

The four beds are divided into two culinary, one medicinal and one sacred. In the former are coriander, rosemary, savoury, fig, marshmallow, marjoram, carroway, mint, parsley, wild thyme, sorrel, mallow, dill and fennel. Ground elder and couch grass, the bane of modern gardens were used as vegetables; ground elder was also used as a cure for gout.

Rosemary or Lavender Sugar

Clean and dry the rosemary or lavendar. Put in a screw topped jar and fill with caster sugar. Shake well and leave for 24 hours. Shake again and leave for a week before use. The sugar gives a delicious flavour to milk puddings, cakes or biscuits.

For medicinal purposes there are white horehound, betony, pennyroyal and rue. The latter was mainly used to neutralize the effects of hemlock which was a popular way to get rid of enemies.

The sacred herbs are the plants we prize today for their scent or decorative properties. French lavender, bay, myrtle, violets, vervain and bear's breeches, otherwise known as Acanthus mollis. These are the beautiful leaves which feature so much in classical architecture and furniture and every Corinthian column has them. The violets and vervain were made into special garlands for festive occasions and flax and nettles which were used in weaving were thought to have a sacred function. In this garden, box hedges separate the beds as they would have done in Hadrian's day.

Walnut and cherry trees were also Roman introductions and these grow in Susie's peaceful garden. The National Thyme Collection is sited here, scores of sweet smelling and subtley coloured cousins of the wild variety. A dedicated plantsman could easily spend a happy day in the verbena scented glasshouse or wandering through the adjoining woodland and there is always an enthusiastic and knowledgeable person on hand to give advice.

Continuing up steep Walwick bank, we make a brief detour from all thing Roman and turn right to Simonburn and Nunwick. Here in the early 1700's lived Margaret Allgood, wife of the squire. Like all well placed ladies of her day she was responsible for a large household staff and had to choose menus for entertaining and supervise her cook.

Margaret's interest however, went very much beyond the usual involvement and she wrote out all her recipes in a beautiful, legible script in a leather bound book. This survives today giving a wonderful insight into the sort of food that was available at that time and the elaborate and lengthy preparations needed to cook it.

What is amazing is the variety of ingredients, attention to detail and the sophistication of many of the dishes. Her use of herbs and spices make much of the unadventurous, quick, easy and boring cooking of today seem very dull. Time, the lack of it, is a modern problem and no doubt Mrs Allgood spent most of hers at home. With our modern equipment and easy shopping we could cut the more time consuming corners and produce many of her excellent recipes with very little trouble. We have a valuable heritage of good English cooking in books like Margaret Allgood's which deserves to be resurrected.

The following come from Margaret Allgoods Receipt Book of 1720

To Stew Ducks In Butter

Take ducks and season them well with mace, cloves, pepper and salt. fill their belly's with thyme, winter savoury, parsley and onions. Put them into your butter and cover them close and set them on the fire. When they are stewed, take the herbs in it. Put the ducks on a dish and take the butter they were stewed in out very easy and take the gravy which is at the bottom of the dish and put it to the sauce with some whole pepper and pour your sauce on them and serve.

To make Mantaloons

Take a neck of mutton, cut it into steaks. Season them put before the fire to broil them. Take a little forced meat with some anchovies in it and lay some over the steaks and wrap them up in white paper and broil them again.

To Stew Oysters

Take your oysters and a little liquer, half a pint of white wine, two blades of mace, a nutmeg. Shred a little marjoram, two shallots, two anchovies and let them stew half a quarter of an hour then put in two yolks of egg, a little butter garnished with sippits of lemon and barberries.

(It is interesting to note how closely this 18th century recipe resembles the Roman way to stew oysters. The use of herbs and spices and salty things like anchovies to add flavour is very Romanesque.)

The hamlet of Nunwick, where Margaret lived was owned in the 1300's by the Heron family. In 1681 Margaret Heron brought the family into grave disrepute by horseracing on Sundays and entertaining the local gentlemen to music at her manor house, thus preventing them from going to church.

They were all taken to a church court by the Reverend Allgood, whose family bought the village in 1740 and built a new manor, designed by William Adam, the father of the more famous Robert. It remains a superb building surrounded by a lovely mature garden and woodland.

Simonburn is also a most attractive village arranged around a green. The thirteenth century church of St Mungo was restored in the 1700's and has a fine array of Saxon and later interior architectural features and stained glass.

A very old tombstone is inscribed with the verse;

Tired of travelling through this world of sin,
At length I'm come to Nature's Common Inn
In this dark place here, for to rest a night
In hopes to rise, that Christ may give me sight.

80

The parish once covered over one hundred square miles stretching from the wall to Liddesdale on the Scottish border. The Vicarage is famous for its ancient three seater lavatory, which would have been ideal for Goldilock's three bears as there is a big one, a medium sized one and a very small one.

Returning to the B6318 we are plunged straight back into Roman times. The road runs straight for many miles, high and bleak and lonely. One misty morning a little group of school children were overwhelmed by the sight of a Roman soldier patrolling the Wall. It was not a ghost but a marvellously imaginative history teacher dressed for the part. Little has changed along this route since Roman times however, the fertile valley of South Tyne lies to the left and to the right the protective whinsill escarpment. There can be few such uninhabited areas in the county or country.

On each side of the road are the remains of Roman forts, turrets and milecastles and in the very middle of all three is the farmstead of **Sewingshields**. The farmhouse is built from the massive stones of the wall, parts of turret thirty four and an inscribed centurial stone rest in the farmyard. Today, visitors from all over the world come here for Bed and Breakfast with Lyn Murray and her family and enjoy living history and home cooking at first hand.

In 1266 a manor house stood here. In 1415 it was listed as a castle which by 1541 had deteriorated to a tower. It was still worthy of Sir Walter Scott's notice as he mentions it as "The Castle of the Seven Shields" in his poem "Harold the Dauntless". In Tomlinson's super guide to the county he writes that King Arthur and his court are thought to lie sleeping in a nearby cave, waiting to be released from a spell by one who will blow a bugle and cut a garter with a sword from the stone. One shepherd is said to have got as far as cutting the garter but forgot to blow the bugle, causing the desperate king to exclaim;

O, woe betide that evil day
On which this witless wight was born,
Who drew the sword, the garter cut,
But never blew the bugle-horn.

The followers of the Round Table are presumably still sitting there somewhere waiting for a less witless wight to free them.

The Murray family who have been farmers for over four hundred years, came to Sewingshields from Scotland in 1940. On the bare white hills they run a traditional herd of White Shorthorn cattle. These lovely animals are quite rare these days. They were a very popular dual purpose breed, producing meat and milk, but fell out of favour because they didn't give the vast amounts of lean (often coarse and tasteless) meat which the imported breeds can pile on so quickly.

They also have the furry eared Black Galloways, so wild that at calving time they protect their young like tigers and have to be warily treated. The cross-breds are called Blue Greys because of their pretty blue roan colouring and the Murray's fatten the bullocks for meat. Their pure bred Blackface flock is

81

famous in the area and their ewe lambs, washed and dressed for the sales, the bonniest and best.

Sewingshields is certainly a good place to get a taste of Northumbria at all levels. Lyn, who learned many of her cookery skills from her mother-in-law Tibbie, provides breakfast and an evening meal. As many of her guests are walkers, by the time they arrive they simply want to curl up in comfort and enjoy their supper.

Lyn buys all her ingredients locally, those that she doesn't grow herself. Home cured bacon, sausages and lamb come from Andy Shield's at Haydon Bridge but all the vegetables, potatoes, carrots, beans, parsnips, onions, leeks and courgettes, raspberries, rhubarb, blackcurrants and every kind of herb come from the Sewingshield garden. A triumph indeed on such cold, high ground.

Breakfast might be bacon and egg, sausage, mushrooms, tomato and fried bread, with porridge, toast and Lyn's own jams, marmalade or lemon curd. Steak and Kidney pie is a favourite for dinner, or chicken with fresh tarragon or pork with onion sauce. Mrs Murray senior is the expert for brown scones and shortbread. This is traditional Northumbrian food and hospitality at its best.

Only a mile or so further on is the impressive Roman Fort of Housesteads, the British Pompeii. It is one of the most popular sites on the Wall and rightly so.

In the time of Agricola AD77-84, Housesteads was only a turret, but when Hadrian arrived in AD 120 to build the Wall, it was transformed into a fort where 1,000 men from the First Cohort of Tungarians from Belgium were stationed with their families living in the adjoining civilian settlement.

Even though the remains are extensive, it is hard to imagine over 3,000 people living here and being able to find adequate food in such an austere setting.

Good food was vital to the morale and stamina of the troops and evidence suggests that they lived amazingly well. A butcher's shop would be supplied with local beef, mutton, goat and pork. Housesteads is near the gateway at Knag End which allowed trade from the North. Large quantities of meat were cured and kept in the granaries.

The Romans domesticated Barnacle geese and Mallard ducks, keeping them in pens and feeding them with grain. They also kept hares and rabbits in special Leporaria. New born bunnies, laurices, were a special delicacy.

Nothing was wasted. Snails were collected and fed on a mixture of milk and wine until they were so fat that they couldn't retreat into their shells, at which point they were fried in butter. In wooded areas even the dear dormouse was at risk. When caught they were fattened to a suitable size and then backed into little earthenware pots. Here they continued, unsuspectingly to guzzle acorns and chestnuts, thinking how good life was. As soon as they filled their little pots it was off to the oven to be stewed.

To complement all the meat, huge amounts of herbs were eaten, causing a contemporary writer to exclaim "that is why life is so short for men in this world, since they stuff their bellies with suchlike herbs, fearful to speak of. Men will eat herbs which cows leave alone!"

At Walltown, chives brought here by the Romans still flourish in the nooks and crannies. Sir Walter Scott, who seems to have an appropriate quotation for everything, wrote;

Take these flowers, which purple waving
On the ruined ramparts grew
Where, the sons of freedom braving,
Rome's Imperial standards flew.

To provide sport as much as meat, the camp commandant and his favourites no doubt spent time in pursuit of wild deer and boar. The latter was often boiled in salt water and served with highly flavoured sauces. Hares were chased with hounds and every sort of bird from herons down were trapped and netted.

At Vindolanda, the fort near Chesterholm, fascinating new evidence has emerged from writing tablets. This shows that the prefect here, one Flavius Cerialis, lived the life of a country gentleman, hunting and throwing parties. A list of his equipment includes small nets for catching thrushes and large dragnets for swans. These would have been served upon his new dinner service which the tablets tell us, was ordered from London. His Batavian soldiers did not have such a jolly time and a letter from a frustrated officer reads "The Comrades have no beer. I ask that you order some to be sent".

The excellent museum here has a reconstruction of a Roman kitchen, showing the basic utensils needed by a Roman soldier's wife. The hearth is raised with a grid resting over the flames on which stew pots frying pans and pieces of meat could be laid to cook.

Cattle, sheep and goats were kept here. The cattle were the small Celtic shorthorns, the ancestors of the breed kept at Sewingshields. The goats and sheep were milked, their skins tanned and wool and goat hair used respectively for clothing and making ropes and tent covers. Goat kids were often roasted whole. All in all the Romans were better fed and better organised than the natives who scratched around trying to make a living on their isolated farms.

In later centuries what is now East Twice Brewed Farm, was an inn catering for the busy pack horse service between Newcastle and Carlisle. It was built in 1776 and known as The Twice Brewed Ale.

A brave old man called William Hutton made a journey along the Wall in 1801. He stayed here and wrote of the huge appetites of the carriers. Fifteen of them sat down to "Pudding as big as a peck measure" and a joint of beef "perhaps equal to half a calf".

William watched as "every piece went down as though there was no barricade to the throat," and they washed it down with ale like "a bowl ladling water out of a well." A new Twice Brewed Inn now stands on the junction of the Road to Vindolanda and Haltwhistle.

We end our journey appropriately at The Milecastle Inn, where Margaret and Ralph Paine use many of the same local ingredients favoured by their Roman predecessors.

The Milecastle is justly renowned for its soups and game dishes. Al the vegetables are bought fresh locally and the meat comes from Mr Walton, a Bellingham butcher. Herbs from Susie White are used in profusion. The Paines tried to grow their own but were defeated by the cold winds. The only exception was the horseradish, which continues to thrive and produces endless fresh horseradish sauce.

The choice of soup is extensive. Leek and potato, curried parsnip, orange and carrot, tomato and mint, chicken and leek and celery and wine are just a few. The game is equally varied. Wild boar is increasingly popular and Ralph makes a mean wild boar and duck pie. He prefers the Eastern European variety at the moment as he finds it has a better flavour. Venison, pheasants, rabbit and pigeons are available in season and Hare, so favoured with the Romans and not often found on menus is a house speciality. What better place for a flagging "foodie" to enjoy a memorable meal.

Trail Four

Cheviot
Picnic

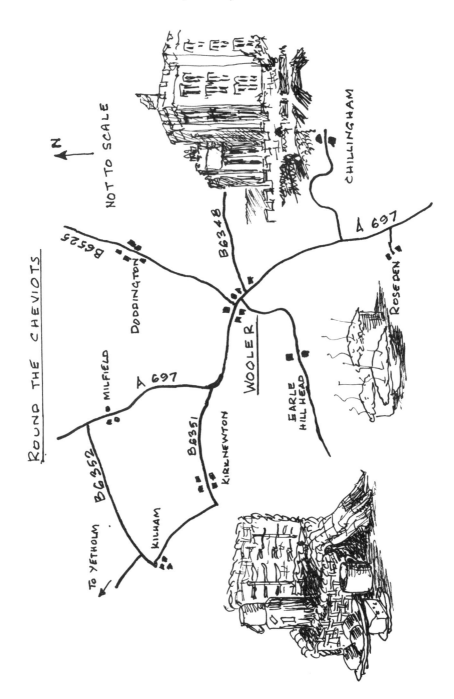

NOT TO SCALE

N

ROUND THE CHEVIOTS

B6525

DODDINGTON

B6348

CHILLINGHAM

A 697

ROSEDEN

MILFIELD

A 697

WOOLER

EARLE HILL HEAD

B6351

KIRKNEWTON

B6352

KILHAM

TO YETHOLM

Cheviot Picnic

No tour of Northumbria would be complete without the chance to experience the "charm of the Cheviots". To do this we venture some way up the Langleeford valley in the Cheviot foothills and also follow the river Glen in the College Valley. For the fit "foodie" who wishes to get a marvellous view to the coast, Cheviot can be climbed from both these approaches. But be warned, follow your map, wear the right clothing and don't take chances if the weather is bad. It is still a wild area, hence its charm.

What better way to start a serious culinary campaign than with a delicious cup of coffee and home made cakes at Mrs Anne Walton's Farm Shop and Restaurant at Roseden, just off the A697, five miles south of Wooler?

Several years ago when many farmer's and their wives looked to new enterprises to supplement falling prices, Mrs Walton decided to put her years of experience cooking for a large family and a formal training at Kirkley Hall, to good use. With the help of the shepherd's wife, she began to bake vast quantities of scones, cakes and biscuits, all made with butter and farm eggs.

A growing range of their own home produced beef and lamb as well as pork and home made sausage from a neighbour, can be bought fresh or in special made to order "freezer packs", which are snapped up by discerning visitors from "the Town", who appreciate real country flavour.

A wonderful variety of pies - steak, chicken, lamb and game, all made with local produce and jams, jellies and pickles, with fruit mainly from her garden, are also made by the tireless Anne who is occasionally spotted, in a flurry of flour, as she dashes between shop and kitchen.

The tiny restaurant, cosily converted from a range of traditional stone buildings, offers coffee, light lunches and teas every day. Dinner is available on Thursday and Friday evenings, but must be booked in advance. The traditional Sunday Lunch is exactly that, Mrs Walton serving the sort of meal that well fed farmers have looked forward to on Sunday through generations past.

Anne Walton has to bake furiously every day to satisfy her customers. Traditionally farmers wives baked on Fridays or Saturdays, so that there were plenty fresh scones and cakes for Sunday visitors. The only day of the week when farmers had time for a little social life.

Seed cake, eaten on such occasions, is a very old recipe dating back to pagan times when it was baked especially at the end of sowing to ensure a good harvest. the farmer is taking no chances when he tells his wife to make all these dishes containing grains for an "apres sowing" celebration.

"Wife, sometime this week, if that all things go clear, An end of wheat sowing we make for this year. Remember you therefore, though I do not it not, The seed cake, the patties, the furmenty pot."

Seed Cake

8 ozs flour	*4 ozs sugar*
4ozs butter	*2 eggs*
2 ozs carroway seeds	*1 tbspn milk salt*

Mix flour and salt and rub in fat. Add sugar and seeds and mix. Make a well in centre and add well beaten eggs and milk. Beat well and put in a greased and floured 8" tin and bake at 350F for approximately 45 minutes

Before proceeding to Wooler, a short detour to Chillingham is too good to be missed. Take the very minor road off the A697 almost opposite the Roseden road end and follow the signs. Chillingham is a very small place but has three major attractions, the famous wild, white cattle, and a magnificent castle and church.

The castle is approached by a two mile carriage drive, lined with mature lime trees. The gates inserted in the park walls are most impressive and lead to an even more awesome facade. First built in the 12th century it was fortified in the 14th. It is quadrangular in shape with four solid towers connected with the 17th century building in an Italian style. In the courtyard the main apartments are reached by a stone staircase.

The castle has always been owned by the Grey family. One branch, the Earls of Tankerville and their decendants recently handed the castle over to Sir Humphrey Wakefield who is related to the Greys by marriage. Sir Humphrey has given the castle a new lease of life and restored the beautiful Italian gardens created by Sir Jeffrey Wyatville. Both are now open to the public.

In the village is the 12th century church of St Peter with its original Norman doorway and in a side chapel is the outstanding altar-tomb of the knight Sir Ralph Grey and his wife Elizabeth of Ravensworth. The quality of the carving is exceptional and the detail on the serene faces so realistic.

The most ancient inhabitants of Chillingham are without doubt the cattle. There are many theories about their origin. It has been suggested that they were brought over with William the Conqueror or are the remains of an enclosed herd of native wild cattle. Research on their skeletons have shown them to be primitive, unique and unchanged since their enclosure in the 13th century.

There is a mysterious quality about these animals, which have survived without human interference other than being given hay, for over 600 years. The herd now safely numbered in forties have evolved their own strict rules for survival. Despite the total lack of new blood, the herd is not inbred because of their hierarchy. Only the King bull mates with the cows and only the strongest bull in the herd achieves this position through fighting off opposition. Only a mature bull of eight or nine years may be king and that only for two years, so that a bull will never breed with his daughters. Some males therefore never have the chance to breed and they and the deposed kings form bachelor groups away from the main herd.

Chillingham Bull & Calf

In appearance they are also unique. They are white with black muzzles, have white horns with black upturned tips and the insides of their ears are red roan. If a calf is touched by a human the herd will kill it and every new calf has to be introduced to the herd at a few days old for approval. Any sickly or deformed animals will also be destroyed. Their discipline is incredible.

At one time the herd was so numerous that animals were regularly killed for meat. The bulls which weigh 35 - 45 stones and the cows 25 - 35, provided finely marbled lean meat with an excellent flavour. When a kill was made all the locals flocked on horse and foot to partake. Horsemen shed off one bull and a marksman shot it. It was said on one occasion to take thirty shots to finally subdue it.

In 1872 the visiting Prince of Wales, sportingly concealed in a haycart massacred the King bull. The carcase provided an ox roast for the less well off on the estate.

Following the A697 again, a few minutes drive finds the small town of Wooler. As its name suggests it was once a thriving centre of the wool trade and as early as 1199 was granted a market charter, shipping wool to all parts of the kingdom and also abroad; becoming one of the four wealthiest towns in the country.

"Wild and Romatic" was how Sir Walter Scott described the countryside around Wooler when he stayed there in 1791. It has become well known since then as a healthy holiday centre where fell walking, bird watching or simply enjoying wonderful farmhouse fare could be indulged. Sir Walter's happy memories of "delicious heath-fed mutton, barn door fowl, and trouts half a yard in length." can be revived today with the wealth of produce from local shops and restaurants or direct from the farms.

At the south end of the long main street, opposite the market cross, is Mr Bryson's tiny bakery which remains virtually unchanged since it was established over a hundred years ago by the present owners great grandfather.

Original recipes are still used for the rich fruit granny loaves and the Baker's biscuits, once called Penny biscuits and bought by all the local children on their way home from school. Today oatcakes are made by Mr Bryson's granddaughter, Moira, exactly as they were in 1882, with local oats from just over the border near Berwick.

Sadly the days have gone when the bread was delivered to the door, first by a smart pony and trap and later by a succession of polished vans. However it is still rewarding to leave the shop with a still warm, yeasty loaf carefully wrappped in tissue paper by Mr Bryson.

T.R. Johnson, the butcher's is another family business where quality and tradition count and great pride is taken in using as much locally reared meat as possible. Wooler is set in the heart of an area famous for its good animal husbandry. The valleys produce excellent grass fed beef, while on the hills run the herds of hardy Blackface ewes and sturdy little white Cheviots. The sweet flavour of the lamb owes much to the variety of natural herbs and grasses on which they graze.

Paul Johnson explained that his best customers are the farmers who supply him with their own stock; a firm indication of 'the proof of the pudding'. Pudding is in fact a speciality of the shop. Made only in Northumberland, White Pudding, a traditional mixture of bacon, pickled beef, mint and seasoning is sold here as well as Haggis and a strange sausage shaped object called a Bung, which is really just a Haggis in disguise!

All these are made on the premises, as are home cured Bacon, potted meat, cooked ham and a Thin Pork sausage in natural casing, the last two made to a well guarded secret recipe. Paul's customers know exactly what they want and he has to provide a huge range of cuts and joints that are never seen in a supermarket. Convenience food has been slow to reach Wooler and some of the slower cooking cuts which retain all their flavour are available here and well worth trying.

Across the road is The Good Life Shop which stocks a wonderful selection of unusual and wholesome fare. Timothy and Diana Sharpe the owners, are brave pioneers in the fight against the bureaucracy which often prevents us from buying the tasty home produced fare we would like.

In a recent campaign, Diana, dressed as a chicken, delivered a petition to a government department, protesting about the rules regarding the production and packaging of free range eggs. It is sad that such measures tend to wipe out the small, careful producers, thus limiting consumer choice and leaving the market open only to large commercial enterprises.

Flavour is still surely an essential ingredient in the pleasure of eating. Part of the joy of travelling is being able to sample local specialities, be it in China or the Cheviots and the Sharpes eagerly seek out interesting delicacies from Northumbrian producers. These range from sheep and cow's cheese from the Redesdale Dairy, near Otterburn, to heather honey from the Chainbridge Honey Farm in Berwickshire, which also makes a wonderful side-line of "bee based" products including hand cream and furniture polish! Free range duck and hen eggs, jams and marmalades, organic flour and oatmeal, all from the Wooler area jostle for shelf space with oils, herbs and spices from more exotic locations in this imaginative and well stocked shop.

Before leaving Wooler, a visit to Mrs Sylvia Armstrong's Farming and Household Museum is a must for anyone with even the slightest interest in Northumberland's rural past, especially food and how it was prepared.

Three miles out of the town on the Langleeford road which leads into the Cheviot foothills, is a sign to Earle Hill Head. Here Sylvia, her husband Charlie and their son William farm three thousand acres of some of the most beautiful land in the country.

This is mainly a livestock farm with suckler cows which produce calves for beef. The sheep are Swaledales which are crossed with a Blue Faced Leicester ram to produce "mule" lambs, the males or "wethers" being fattened while the ewe lambs are sold for breeding.

There is a long running battle among Northern farmers as to whether the Swaledale or Blackface sheep is the best. To the uninitiated, a sheep is a sheep and one might be forgiven for mistaking a Swale for an anaemic Blackface. To those "in the know", the difference is critical and a topic for much animated discussion in the pub on an evening.

According to one expert, a good Swale must have a narrow mouth for nibbling between the rocks when grazing on the mountains. The face wool must be thick as coconut matting and the tail, long, thick and woolly to withstand icy blasts. The pro "Blackie" faction however have been heard to say that the Swale is so narrow at the front that both its forelegs come out of the same hole!

Despite her involvement in this thriving farm Sylvia has found time to develop her passion for collecting into a fascinating museum filled with relics of farmlife as it used to be. Particularly in teresting are the range of Victorian kitchen implements which must rival anything Mrs Beeton might have used The spiked ham stand which allows the joint to be carved more easily, the Tongue press and a device for stretching sides of bacon, would not be out of place in a torture chamber. But there are also the most delicate little tins for hand made chololate and beautifully carved wooden butter moulds which shaped the finished butter and left an imprint, often a cow, or a sheaf of corn, on the surface.

Preparing meals at the turn of the century was not only time consuming but extremely difficult, as the ingenuity and incongruity of many of these objects show. It is also obvious that food was taken very seriously and not only had to be cooked to perfection but had also to look attractive.

Sylvia herself is an excellent cook, as her Farmhouse Bed and Breakfast guests will testify. When her daughter Barbara was married recently, she and her mother cooked their own lamb and turkeys for the reception to recipes from their vast collection and "borrowed" the beatiful Victorian glass and china from the Museum to serve it on.

Mrs Armstrong's Favourite Lemon Pudding

4 fresh Farm eggs   *4 lemons*
large tin condensed milk   *2 ozs caster sugar*
$^1/_2$ pint thick farmhouse cream

Whip sugar and egg yolks together until creamy. Add cream, milk, lemon juice and finely grated rind and fold together. Gently fold in well beaten egg whites. Pour mixture into a shallow container and freeze. to serve cut into squares and decorate with fresh mint leaves.

95

At Earle Farm, just a mile from the Armstrongs on the return journey to Wooler, another enterprising lady, Sarah Dodds, is producing pork from her small herd of outdoor pigs. The nucleus of the herd consists of four Tamworth sows which she brought home in her trunk as tiny piglets, when she returned from college.

They say that no part of a pig is wasted. This recipe seems to prove the point!

Pigs Pettitoes

Pigs liver, heart and feet	*sprigs thyme*
1 onion thin	*pepper and salt*
slice bacon	*butter*
mace	*flour*
6 peppercorns	*1pt good gravy*

Put liver, heart and pettitoes in a pan with the bacon and mace. Simmer for 1 hour. Remove heart and liver. Stew feet for further 30 mins with chopped onion till tender. Add minced liver, thicken with butter and flour. Put mince on warmed dish. Split feet and arrange on toasted bread. Pour over gravy and serve.

The Tamworth is a rare old English breed, with pink, freckled skin covered in wispy ginger hair, rather similar to a recent leader of the Opposition. Allowing the pigs to run freely outside, where they can indulge their natural instincts to forage, greatly improves the quality of the meat.

Sarah regularly supplies a butcher in Jesmond, Newcastle, but also sells direct from the farm and is happy to provide whatever a customer might want, given prior notice.

To the north of Wooler lies the Glendale and College Valley, where there are many ideal places to enjoy a picnic. Perhaps on the banks of the river Glen, bright with vivid orange and yellow clumps of mimulus and blue water forget-me-nots during the Summer.

A very large picnic took place here in AD627 and is commemorated by a plaque which marks the site of the palace of Edwin of Northumbria at Gerfrin.

Edwin was the first Christian king of Northumbria and in this fertile valley hundreds of men, women and children gathered for thirty six days while Paulinus, the Bishop of York, baptised them in the river.

Large gatherings still occur in the valley and each year, at Kirknewton village hall on January 25th, up to a hundred men and women from all around come to celebrate "Burns Night". This annual ritual to honour the poet Robbie Burns, takes place up and down the country, but Northumberland, being so close to the Scottish border, is particularly enthusiastic.

The high spot of the evening is the entrance of the Haggis, accompanied by music from the Bagpipes. It is then welcomed by the Master of Ceremonies who recites Burns' wonderful "Address to a Haggis"....

"Fair fa' your honest, sonsie face,
Great chieftain of the pudding-race
Aboon them a' ye take your place,
Painch, tribe or thairm
Weel are ye wordy o' a grace
As lang's my arm.

The groaning trencher there ye fill,
Your hurdies like a distant hill,
Your pin wad help to mend a mill in time of need,
While thro your pores the dews distil like amber bead.

After several more verses of praise, just as the Haggis is beginning to relax and enjoy the party, it is attacked with a dagger and served out to all the guests, with liberal helpings of mashed potatoes and "neeps" the local name for turnips, and even more liberal helpings of good whisky. After supper, more whisky is circulated and the evening continues with poetry and song until the early hours.

The influence of the Scots is also to be seen in the tiny church of St Gregory the Great, opposite the village hall. To the left of the chancel arch is a carved stone relief from around the tenth century. It depicts the well known event of the Adoration of the Magi. But look carefully and you will see that the three kings are not wearing Eastern dress but kilts! No doubts they are bearing porridge and oatcakes as more practical presents than frankincense and myrrh.

The rest of the church is worthy of further notice with its wide variety of architectural styles dating from the Saxon or Norman times up to its major refurbishment in the 1860's. The churchyard, nestling under the hills and protected by a pair of inquisitive peacocks, contains the grave of the Victorian, Josephine Butler, one of the first and most effective campaigners for women's rights in days when feminism was unheard of.

Still following the B6351, look out for a silhouette of a black bull at Kilham. Here there is an invitation to take the road into the hills, with only the lapwing and curlew for company. At Kilham Farm in the National Park, the Goodson family, who have been landowners here for generations, wished to share the beauty of this particular area and have devised an excellent 5 kilometre walk. Leaflets are available in the car park with information about the crops, domestic animals and wildlife which can be seen on the farm.

Sir Mark Goodson still runs a herd of pure Aberdeen Angus cattle here. This compact, jet black breed is now quite rare because of the popularity of the French Charolais and Limousin cattle. This is because the health conscious consumer tends to prefer the very lean meat which French breeds provide. However, for sheer taste and texture, there is nothing to beat the Aberdeen Angus. Because the fat is distributed in a marbled pattern throughout the meat, it cooks to perfection. The steaks are especially good and very hard to find in ordinary butchers but the Farm to Freeze shop in Wooler is occasionally supplied by Sir Mark with cattle from this herd.

In times past this valley was home not only to the settled farmers but a large shifting population of "Egyptians" or gipsies, who had their own special cuisine.

Yetholm, the village at the head of the valley was home to the famous Faa family, from whom the gipsy "King" or "Queen" was often chosen. Johnny Faa, self styled "Lord and Erle of littel egipt" was in correspondence with James IV in the 1540's and the last coronation which took place in 1898, crowned Charles Faa Blythe, a direct descendant. "Meg Merrilees" the gypsy of Sir Walter Scott's famous novel "Guy Mannering" was inspired by another Yetholm gypsy, Jean Gordon.

Their legal business was dealing in earthenware pots and mugs, hence their local name of "muggers" or more romantically "lads o' the heather". They also made and sold willow baskets and heather besoms and were generally undeserving of their dubious reputation.

Gypsies at Wooler 1890

99

Meg Dodd's Gypsy Soup 1826

1 lb trimmings & bones from   *part of bird, hare, rabbit etc*
venison or any game   *per person*
3 carrots,   *6 small onions*
3 turnips,   *1 head of celery*
3 onions   *6 potatoes*
4 pts water   *small white cabbage*
peppercorns   *$^1/_2$ lb mushrooms*
parsley   *seasoning*

Most of these ingredients were probably there for the taking. Everything to put into a large cauldron and simmered over an open fire.

Zingaro Gypsy Ham

1 lb ham
1 tbspn vinegar
2 tbspn brown bread crumbs
2 ozs butter

Cut ham into neat pieces. Heat butter and fry ham. Remove and add crumbs to the butter. Fry for a few seconds, add vinegar, reheat and pour over ham.

Their poaching skills ensured a varied diet of pheasant, partridge, trout and salmon, but such game was plentiful as were the wild fruits, blaeberries and hazelnuts which they gathered with little harm to the countryside.

In their methods of cooking the gypsies were also extremely practical. A favoured way of roasting feathered game, a chicken or on occasion, a hedgehog, was to roll the unfortunate creature in clay before baking it in the fire. When done, all that was needed was to peel off the clay and with it the feathers or prickles, thus saving all the bother of plucking.

Marriage between members of the community was equally down to earth. All that was needed to bind the union was to break a whole new cheese over the heads of the happy couple. A tempting and simple alternative to to days expensiveand elaborate rituals!

Turning onto the B6352 at Kilham the road passes the hamlet of Howtel where the remains of a large 16th century tower. This was a favourite point for troops to gather before embarking on a jolly pillage over the border into Scotland.

All around this area the deadly skirmishes of the battle of Flodden Field were won and lost. James IV of Scotland, encouraged by the French to invade England, reached Flodden in Septmenber 1513 and rested on the site of an ancient British camp.

Unlike the English they were well provisioned with "plenteable, beef, mutton, salfysshe and cheese", probably plundered from nearby farms. However it did not prevent them from suffering a grievious defeat. 10.000 Scottish soldires, the King and his bastard son fell at the hands of the Earl of Surrey, giving rise to the haunting Flodden lament-

"We'll hear nae mair lilting at our ewe milking,
Women and bairns are heartless and wae,
Sighing and moaning on ilka green loaning
The Flowers of the Forest are a' wede away.

The route rejoins the A697 at Milfield, where Josephine Butler was born in 1828, one of the ten children of a prosperous farmer, John Grey. This fertile area was once totally submerged after the Ice Age. In later years it was taken over by broom bushes and a farming journal of the 18th century reports that a mare, which was lost in the broom, eventually emerged with a foal! The bushes were finally cleared through the efforts of the Culley brothers, who werefamous agricultural improvers. Broom does have some use and the flowers can be used either as a dye for the old custom of colouring hens eggs for Easter or to make delicious Broom Wine.

Broom Wine

1 gallon water	*2 lemons*
3 lbs lump sugar	*2 oranges*
1 gallon broom flowers rind &	*2 tbspns yeast*
juice	

Boil sugar and water together with lemon and orange rinds for $^1/_2$ *hour. Cool to lukewarm and pour over flowers, picked from their stalks. Add lemon and orange juice. Stir in yeast and allow to ferment for 3 days. Put in a clean dry cask and allow to work for one week to ten days, filling up as required. Then stop up closely and keep for six months. The wine is best made during May, when the flowers are at their freshest.*

At North Doddington Farm, a few miles East of Wooler, Neill Maxwell is bringing a family tradition very much up to date with his newly developed Berwick cheese.

His grandparents, who were dairy farmers in Ayrshire and Dumfriesshire, made their own cheese and fifty years on Neill is doing the same, building on their knowledge and expertise. He has spent the last two years completing his dairy, finding the right equipment and experimenting to find exactly the right sort of cheese.

From his 200 strong herd of Holstein and Normandy cows he is making an unpasteurised Gouda type with a smooth texture and full flavour, which will be properly matured for six months before sale. This process is too often neglected in modern cheeses. Methods are used to speed up maturation, but nothing is the same as waiting patiently until nature has done its work to perfection.

It takes courage and determination to bring a new product to the market. Satisfying all the E.C rules is in itself a nightmare. To make something unique to this area is also admirable and deserving of support. The Good Life Shop in Wooler will be the first stockists of what promises to become an excellent cheese.

After such serious exploring, a meal at Hooty's Restaurant at West Weetwood, is a further opportunity to enjoy local produce, especially seafood while looking out onto the hills and valleys of Glendale. All the meat comes from nearby farms and the scallops, salmon and lobster from the Northumbrian coast. Even oysters from a new bed near Holy Island are available.

In March, for a very short season Gull's eggs are on the menu. These can only be obtained by special licence from certain estates and are a rare gourmet treat.

Ashley Fiddes, the owner and chef, makes a superb Game Pie with the wealth of teal, mallard, partridge, hare, rabbit and venison that abound in this area. Cooked in stout with mushrooms, onions and seasoning, topped with puff pastry, it is a firm favourite.

A Farm Shop, open during the season, supplies game, meat, honey and jams and from Easter, weather permitting, there are barbecue facilities in the pleasant orchard for those who prefer to do their own cokking. A small Garden centre, clothes and antique shop provide further interest.

Trail Five
Farne Island
Fish Stew

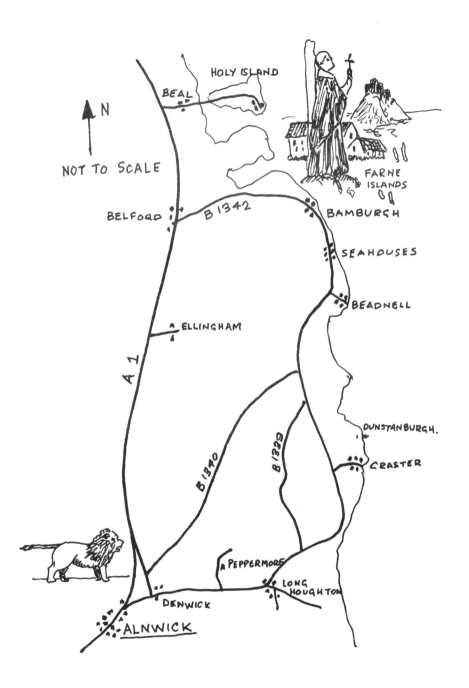

Farne Islands Fish Stew

This tour tries to capture the rough beauty of the Northumbrian coast. In an area blessed with saints and beset by sinners, we visit the bird encrusted Farnes, the Cradle isle of St Aidian and sample the harvest of the sea.

We start our journey in Alnwick to give a sense of the still feudal and medieval character of this part of the world. The site where the castle now stands may well have been an ancient British settlement, ideally placed above the river. The Saxons who gave it the name A'lain Wick, the Town of the Clear Water, were displaced by the followers of William the Conquerer, and Yvo de Vescy, a Norman Baron, built his castle here in 1096.

It was described as a "munitissium castellum" in 1135 and has remained so ever since. The once great Percy family, who came here with William, took over the castle in 1309 and were in residence, wise custodians of the county until the death of the tenth Duke.

The fifth Earl, known as "The Magnificent" was a great bon viveur and his Household Book compiled between 1489 and 1527 record how he and his family dined.

At this time there were 166 people in the Earl's entourage and a allowance was made for the possibility of providing for at least fifty visitors daily. Twopence hapenny per person was set aside for their meat, drink and "firing".

Although the Earl was obviously hospitable, he expected value for his money and his clerks had to make sure that each piece of meat and fish was cut into the optimum number of portions and the total entered in the accounts.

At Halloween "one hundred and nine fat beeves" were bought at thirteen shillings and fourpence each and "twenty four lean beeves" at eight shillings. These were kept in the park to fatten and would last the family for the five months between June and October, which was the only time they ate fresh meat. The rest were slaughtered before Winter and pickled.

To go with all the "beeves", one hundred and sixty gallons of mustard was needed. It does not say if a similar amount of mint sauce was needed for the six hundred and forty seven sheep!

For the Earl himself, "twenty eight veals, twenty five hogs and forty lambs" were purchased. Vegetables were very rarely eaten being looked on as inferior food for peasants and animals.

The day began with mass at six and breakfast at seven o'clock. The Earl deserved to be called Magnificent if only because he was able to consume a quart of beer, the same of wine, red and white herrings, two pieces of salt fish and a dish of sprats or half a chyne of mutton or a whole chyne of beef at such an early hour.

He also fed his twenty seven horses very well, allowing them hay, hard feed of oats and special loaves made of beans. When he travelled which he did with much ceremony, all his own food and bedding and the same for the horses was taken with them as he could not trust the arrangements at the hostelries along the way.

Only two cooks were employed to feed this enormous household. Washing was also kept to a minimum. Forty shillings a year was all that was spent in this department and most of this was for looking after the linen in the chapel.

By 1650 it looks as though there were no cooks at all as half of the six thousand prisoners who were unfortunate enough to be brought to the castle after the battle of Dunbar, died of starvation in eight days.

Tomlinson writes that the restoration of the castle which took place between 1854 and 1865 under the Fourth Duke produced "Kitchens, larders and sculleries which are no less remarkable for their perfect culinary arrangements than for their architectural grandeur. All the ingenious appliances of modern times have been utilised." These included a water powered spit and a hydraulic lift which allowed the food to at least reach the right floor fairly quickly before it was carried along miles of cold corridor to the dining room.

In the nineteeth century the castle gardens provided the array of exotic fruit and vegetables which graced the tables at Victorian Banquets. Apples, pears, cherries, gooseberries, raspberries and currants were established and in the hot houses peaches, pineapples, grapes and rare flowers flourished.

108

The castle today is marvellously intact and houses a unique collection of paintings, porcelain and furniture. It is open every day between Easter and October and there is a Tearoom to provide homemade cakes and scones.

Duke of Northumberland Cake

1 lb butter	*8 eggs*
1 lb sugar	*$^1/_2$ lb currants*
1 lb flour	

Beat the butter thoroughly to a light creamy consistency. Add the sugar and beat again for up to 20 minutes. Add each egg, well beaten, one at a time and stir the cake between each addition. Add the flour and beat again. Finally fold in the fruit. Bake in a moderate oven until well risen and golden brown.

While the inhabitants of the castle enjoyed the pleasures of life, in the adjoining 1250 hectares of Hulne Park two monastic orders were founded. Alnwick Abbey, of which only the ruins remain housed a group of Premonstratensians in 1147 under the indulgent patronage of Eustace Fitz-John.

The White Canons, as they were known seemed to have had quite a jolly time. In 1376 they threw a bash for over a thousand guests. Perhaps in divine retribution the harvest failed and all their sheep and cattle developed a lethal disease and died. The order remained in the park until the dissolution of the monasteries in 1539 and the abbey fell into disrepair.

The Carmelite order made their home in Hulne Abbey in 1240 and lived an austere and contemplative life. To remind them of their mortality they each had a coffin in their cell and dug one spadeful of earth for their graves every morning. They only had two meals a day, never ate meat and often fasted. From the remaining ruins it appears that there was a bakehouse, brewhouse and a mill and a plan of 1817 shows several pheasant aviaries although the latter might be for decoration rather than food.

A lovely tale exists of the monk's method of catching fish. A rare variety of spurge which grows in the park was thrown into the river and the hungry trout swallowed up the pieces. Spurge has extremely hot peppery qualities which caused the fish to gasp and come to the surface, only to be netted by the waiting monks.

There have always been deer in the park and a herd of Fallow still live safely within the walls. They are culled occasionally to prevent tree damage and the venison and other game is sometimes available on application to the Estate Office.

The town of Alnwick was once protected by a wall with four towers. The Bondgate tower still defends the Southern entrance and the Gothic style Pottergate Tower lies to the West. Safe in the centre is the Market Place where food has been traded since 1290.

Here in the Square and under the arcardes in the Shambles were butchers stalls, poultry, eggs and butter. One of the best and cheapest fish markets operated in front of the Town Hall and carriers regularly shipped pork, corn and eggs down to London.

The Marketplace also saw bull baiting which drew huge crowds. At the beginning of this century livestock markets took place here and the town was awash with cattle and sheep.

Alnwick Market C.1900

110

Alnwick today is worth visiting for its history alone, but is rather lacking in exciting finds for the food lover. Trotter's the Baker's provide a range of very good bread, buns and cakes and R.Turnbull, the Butcher buys from local farmers and makes his own sausages and pies.

At Robertson's Prime on the Willowtree trading Estate on the southern outskirts of the town there is value and variety. Here Maragaret and Bill and their son Ian who was once a professional golfer, have built up a good business and always have an excellent supply of fish, game and shellfish.

Most of their white fish comes from Amble and sea bass, one of the more unusual fish is becoming very popular. In the summer fresh langoustines are available as well as crabs, lobster and Lindisfarne Oysters. Wild salmon and sea trout are in season from late April and sometimes fresh eels in August.

Ian is always looking for interesting produce and has venison from local estates and Wild boar from the Yorkshire Dales as well as local rabbits, pigeons, grouse, partridge, pheasant and occasionally woodcock and snipe.

Game Pudding

1 $^1/_2$ lbs suet crust pastry	*1 tbsp finely chopped parsley*
$^1/_2$l b rump steak or vension	*and thyme*
1 pheasant or 2 partridge	*$^1/_2$ lb mushrooms*
2 grouse or 2 pigeons jointed	*2 glasses red wine*
seasoned flour	*1 pt stock*

Line a pudding basin with suet crust. Dip meat and joints in flour. Put meat and some joints in basin, season add herbs and half the mushrooms, then remaining joints and mushrooms. Pour in wine and some of the stock. Cover with foil or greaseproof and over this tie a cloth or put on a lid. Stand basin in large pan of water, so that water comes 1/2 way up bowl or put in a steamer. Cook for 3 hours adding more boiling water if needed. Turn out on to a hot dish. Make a small hole in crust and add more hot stock before serving.

Partridge Casserole

A brace of old birds	*chopped parsley and thyme*
4 onions	*1 savoy cabbage*
4 rashers of bacon	*$^3/_4$ red wine or cider*
2 carrots	*1oz flour*
pepper and salt	*1 oz butter*

Place an onion inside each bird and a rasher of bacon over the breast. Put them in a large casserole with sliced carrot and onion, remaining bacon diced, seasoning and herbs. Pour over wine or cider and leave overnight. In the morning, cut the cabbage into partridge size quarters and pack round the birds. Fill casserole with enough water to cover all. Cook very slowly at 250F for 4 hours.

Retracing our route back into Alnwick a visit to an unusual shop might be of interest. Barter Books owned by Mary and Stuart Manley, and housed in the picturesque old station is an Aladdin's cave for the avid reader. Here old and obscure Victorian recipe books, first edition Mrs Beeton's and brand new Delia Smiths vie for space with thousands of classics, local history, thrillers and novels. A fire is always burning and there is a comfy sofa, an ever bubbling coffee percolator and homemade biscuits provided for the browser to help themselves. The clever idea, as the name implies, is to bring books to exchange. All the stock, including tapes, records and C.Ds are in good condition and sensibly priced.

Exactly opposite the entrance to Barter Books is the Tenantry column. This 80 foot Doric column surmounted by the Percy Lion, with four more guarding the base is a tribute to a generous and respected man. In the foundations is a glass tube containing the names of 1500 of the Duke of Northumberland's tenants, written on vellum. Each person subscribed to the monument in gratitude for the Dukes kindness in waiving their rents at a time of extreme hardship when crops and livestock had failed. Corn, wine and oil were poured over the stone on the 1st July 1816 and prayers offered. Sadly the Duke, Hugh, died before its completion.

At the foot of the column we take the road to Denwick, turning right in the village towards Longhoughton. On the right is the escarpment of the Great Whinsill at Ratcheugh Crag surmounted by a Gothic folly of a ruined castle, built for the Percy family who find it a perfect place for a picnic.

Peppermoor Farm

To the left of the crossroads is Peppermoor Farm, run by Mick and Prue Smith and the home of "Gourmet Goodies". This must be the most imaginative farm shop in the county, complete with its own smokehouse. The welfare of the animals are of prime importance and no artificial preservatives are used.

In partnership with fellow farmers Frank and Marjorie Vickers and Kate Walker, who has the "smoking" expertise, they are developing an exciting range of smoked local produce and traditional raised crust pies. They also stock jams, marmalade, honey, goats milk and yogurt and cheese, all from Northumbrian suppliers.

Much of the range comes from Prue's herd of Angora crossbred goats from which she produces beautiful cashgora yarn, leather and cured goatskins. Joints of the meat, known as "chevon" are smoked, made into Parma style ham's or sold sliced diced and the smoked liver is ideal for pate's.

The sausages are also excellent, made to Prue's own recipe with herbs from the Peppermoor garden. These include parsley, chives, thyme and tarragon varieties and a small smoked cocktail sausage.

Goats have been farmed in Northumberland since many hundred years B.C providing meat, milk and skins. In Roman times they were well established in upland areas and the great Roman gourmet Apicius was particularly fond of kid meat, roasted on a spit or cooked in a small portable oven called a clibanus.

Apicius' Honeyed Liver

Make honeywater and mix it into beaten eggs and milk. Make incisions in kid's liver and let it absorb the liquid. Then cook in wine, season well with pepper and serve.

Gourmet Goodies' pies continue the old tradition of combining meat with fruit to complement the flavours. Their ham and turkey pie contains kidney and apricots soaked in sherry. The game pie, full of local venison, smoked pheasant, chevon sausage, onions and garlic is blended with blackcurrants drenched in port.

There is also a selection of turkey from the Vicker's farm, sliced smoked breast, turkey and ham roll made to an old family recipe and crown of turkey and Northumbrian Cured bacon.

Local salmon, trout, haddock and mussels are smoked on the premises and customers can make arrangements to have their own goodies smoked.

Prue's Chevon Herb Sausage Casserole

1tbspn oil	*1 400gr tin tomatoes*
1 large onion	*2 sticks celery, chopped*
1 clove garlic	*1 sliced green pepper*
1tbspn whole grain mustard	*salt,*
3ozs streaky bacon	*freshly ground black pepper*
5oz chicken stock	*bay leaf*
1 lb herb sausage-	
Thyme, tarragon & garlic or	
parsley & chive	

Grill sausages and bacon until golden brown. Fry onion and garlic gently in oil until soft but not brown, stir in mustard, cooked sliced sausage, celery, bacon, tomatoes, pepper, bay leaf and stock. Simmer covered for 20 minutes.

114

One mile further on is the village of Longhoughton. It was once famed for its productive flower and vegetable gardens. Because it is so close to the sea shore it allowed the villages to "donge" their plots with seaweed to increase their fertility. The gardens - not the gardeners!

The mainstays of life here used to be St Peter's Church and the Blue Bell Inn. Unfortunately it often happened that when the sober citizens left their Sunday Service they were confronted by the capers of the decidedly unsober, who had spent the morning at the Inn and came out on purpose to upset the churchgoers. The Duchess of Northumberland was not amused and ordered that the pub be closed down.

The church dating back to the thirteenth century houses the remains of the Market Cross which was rediscovered in a smugglers grave.

Howick Hall, on the road to Craster, is now celebrated for its woods and gardens, especially the carpets of spring daffodils. A tower built in 1416 was the first dwelling here. It was Henry Grey, brother of the first Earl Grey, who built the Hall in 1778.

About this time an article appeared in the "Newcastle Chronicle";

"Monday last was brought from Howick to Berwick to be shipped to London for Sir Henry Grey a pie, the contents whereof are as follows. 2 bushels of flour, 20lbs of butter, 4 geese 2 turkeys, 2 rabbits, 4 wild ducks, 2 woodcocks, 6 snipes, 4 partridges, 2 neats tongues, 2 curlews, 7 blackbirds and 6 pigeons. It was supposed a very great curiosity and was made by Mrs Dorothy Patterson, Housekeeper at Howick. It was near 9' at the circumference, weighs about twelve stones and will take two men to present it at table. It is neatly fitted with a case and four small wheels to facilitate its use to every guest that inclines to partake of its contents."

Pies often contained surprises as this 1660 account records; "And from this pie out skips some Frogs, which makes the Ladies to skip and shriek. Next the pie from whence came the Birds, who by natural instinct, flying at the light do put out the candles, so that what with the Flying Birds and Skipping Frogs, the one above the other, itwill cause much delight and pleasure to the company."

Howick is also associated with the great nineteenth century naturalist Grey of Falloden, who was Foreign Secretary during the 1914-18 war and made the memorable comment "The lights are going out all over Europe.

We also have this family to thank for Earl Grey tea. The story goes that a secret recipe for this fragrant tea scented with oil of the herb Bergamot was passed to a diplomat in Earl Grey's embassy by a Chinese Mandarin, whose life he had saved. Either the Earl pinched the recipe or the diplomat had a very boring or embarrasing name unsuitable for promoting an upmarket tea; we shall never know.

Passing the ancient basalt pele tower built before the Conquest by William de Craucestr **we arrive in the village of Craster**. Despite its summer influx of tourists it maintains the feel of the closely knit fishing community which flourished here as a centre of the herring trade until the early nineteen hundreds.

Perched above the sheltered harbour, where the few brightly coloured fishing boats which work fron here, bob safely in their rocky haven, L. Robson and Sons still produce the famous Craster Kipper.

Allan, whose grandfather started the business, his wife, Kathleen and their son Neill are now at the helm. Robson's kippers are rightly sought after all over the world and orders are regularly recieved from the Gulf, Canada and Australia.

The secret of the flavour lies in the smoking process. This takes place between June and September when the herring are plump and full of oil. Traditionally scores of young women who were employed to gut the fish, followed the herring from Yorkshire to Scotland. Now a special splitting machine is used which cleans, washes and dips the fillets in brine.

The fish are hung on tenter sticks and carried into the smokehouses and placed up in the rafters. As many as two and a half thousand might be suspended at a time during the height of the season. Here they remain, literally "on tenterhooks" over the smouldering fires of Whitewood shavings covered by the special oak sawdust. Unlike the strange coloured kippers so often seen in supermarkets, Craster Kippers depend solely on the smoke to give them their colour and flavour.

Herring Lasses on the North East Coast

The little shop sells not only kippers but wonderful oak smoked salmon, whole fresh salmon and sea trout, white fish and shell fish from the Northumberland coast.

In the Restaurant which has stunning views over the harbour and along the dunes to the ghostly ruin of Dunstanburgh Castle, Kathleen specialises in really good fish. Her sandwiches are filled to overflowing with fresh crab, salmon or prawns and the fish and shellfish dishes are always generous, and owe their super flavour to being straight out of the sea.

Mrs Robson's Grilled Craster Salmon

4 salmon steaks	*8 tbspns white wine*
4 lemons	*4 tbspns chopped coriander*
4ozs brown sugar	*olive oil*
4 tbspns chopped dill	*sea salt*

Combine herbs with salt and sugar. Add juice of two lemons and wine. Brush with mixture. Cover in clingfilm and stand for two hours. Brush with oil and grill for one minute each side.

Dunstanburgh Castle

Whatever the weather, and it can sometimes be wonderfully stormy, it is always worth walking the mile or so along the very edge of the sea to Dunstanburgh castle.

Once a terrifying fortress, now a stark ruin, it sits precariously above three sheer cliffs, buffeted by the wild North sea. Simon de Montfort, Earl of Leicester and Baron of Embleton, first saw Dunstanburgh's potential for impregnability in 1257. It was not until Henry III's grandson inherited the land that a massive building was begun in 1313 and fortified three years later.

During three hundred years of bitter Border wars it changed sides five times and was home to John of Gaunt before eventually passing to the Grey family. It is now administered by English Heritage.

Fifteen acres at the South end of the ridge were originally enclosed with buildings to shelter cattle and space to grow corn in times of unrest. Traditionally, nothing was wasted. Even during peaceful times the meat of the toughest old ox was pounded into pastes or put in "mighty broths of beef". Tough cuts were cooked with minced onions and cloves and entrails were used in soups, cooked in broth or served in wine with leeks. The liver, kidney and heart could be braised and even the lungs and spleen were strongly seasoned and con-

118

sumed. The head, tongue, udder and testicles all had their own special recipes, few of which, perhaps mercifully have survived.

The best joints were roasted and a carver employed specifically to dissect them in the correct manner. A sixteenth century book was written on the art of carving, each meat having its own terminology. Accordingly each carver had to know how to;

Breke that dere
Lyfte that swanne
Unbrace that mallarde
Dismembre that heron
Tayme that crab
Undertrance that porpoise
Splat that pike

All of which conjures up jolly pictures that must have thoroughly enlivened medieval mealtimes. The R.S.P.B would nowadays no doubt object to a traditional Sunday dismembre of the heron.

A mile or so along the coast, almost under the shadow of Dunstanburgh, **is Embleton.** The church of the Holy Trinity was built in 1320 on the site of a Norman church and was held under the patronage of Merton College, Oxford. The Vicarage is of interest because of its pele tower, the "Turris de Emylton, built in 1332 and enlarged in 1828 to the design of the famous Newcastle architect, John Dobson.

Embleton has two unusual dovecotes. One of red brick in the vicarage grounds and another, much older, of stone at the South end of the village.
Doves and pigeons, which supplied variety to the diet of the nobility and upper classes during the Winter, were far from popular with the local farmers and gardeners whose grain and seedlings they devoured.

In the fourteenth century the village had a brewing licence and was a centre for grinding corn. The fertile land around was perfect for sheep, many of which were milked for cheesemaking. Sheep cheese was more common then than cow's, the fat content is much higher and it produces a rich, creamy curd. The problem lies in the milking. Small fingers and wrists like the Boston Strangler's are needed. Directing the milk into the pail and not up the sleeve is also an art to be learnt.

Few people make cheese or anything else, on a small scale today because of the Draconian E.U directives on hygiene. Consequently, everything tastes the same and life is very dull. If a consenting adult wants to live dangerously and eat cheese made from unpasteurised milk from a small producer, he should be allowed to do so. Some French cheeses are lifting with microbes, good and bad and taste delicious. The more we live in a sterile environment, eating sterile food the more likely we are to succumb to the tiniest bug. Building up a healthy immunity through gradual acclimatization to such things should be encouraged. What we need is real ale, real bread, real cheese, real food!

Beadnell, as indeed all these coastal village were, was a hotbed of smugglers. In 1762 Customs seized 2,700 gallons of brandy, 400 gallons of rum, 23 hogsheads of wine and numerous cases of tea.

Fishing was the offical business here and in 1788 John Wood founded the Northumberland branch of the British Fisheries. Beadnell was a hectic place in the eighteenth and nineteeth centuries. The harbour was improved and lime from the nearby kilns, sea coal and grain were shipped out. There were also salt pans which provided salt for the tons of herring which were gutted by the Scottish girls who followed the shoals.

In 1828 over a thousand fishermen in one hundred boats sheltered in the harbour during a storm. Few herrings were gutted that night!

Fishing still continues in the same elegant little Northumberland cobles but only one or two of the original Beadnell families like the Dixons and the Douglases are involved. Sea trout, salmon, lobsters and crabs are caught in ever decreasing numbers, while the red tape from a haddock and never leave their centrally heated offices, increase daily. Thus are broken the hearts and the livelihood of the men whose families have braved storms, freezing cold and dirty conditions for generations to make a living from the sea.

On the headland near Ebb's Nook are the remains of a thirteenth century chapel. It was found in 1835 having been covered by sand for many years. It was built on the site of a seventh century church erected at the command of the Saxon Princess Ebba, sister of King Oswald of Northumbria. The church in the centre of the village is also called St Ebba's.

Anglo Saxon times seem to have been either a feast or fast. Fasting was not only good for the soul but a practical way to conserve resources during seasonal shortages. Food and power feasts were looked forward to. The Lord who could provide nourishment for his vassals was usually the most successful.

A woman's lot was fairly grim one unless you were a Princess, like the lucky Ebba. Females spent their lives finding and cooking food for their menfolk, but rarely joined them at meals, eating leftovers and poor quality food. This resulted in very early deaths, usually in childbirth due to malnutrition or deficiency induced disease.

In coastal areas like Embleton, at least fish was available and this provided minerals, oils and vitamins. Food recommended for good blood included "shellfishes, finned fishes, wild hens, all birds that live on the hills, pigeons, half grown pigs, goats flesh and the juice "of peas with honey somewhat peppered".

Seahouses always sounds so romantic and picturesque. Unfortunately these qualities are confined to the harbour and its environs, with its seaweedy smell and glorious views to the Farnes.

In the Winter it is a ghost town of deserted amusement arcades and in the Summer it is heaving with tourists. In Victorian times the elegant mansions on the sea front were owned by or rented to wealthy families from Newcastle who came here for the whole Summer to enjoy the salty air and make sand castles on the miles of unspoilt silver beaches.Huge groups of friends and relations gatheres for elaborate picnics. the following is a recommened menu for such a feast.

Picnic for Forty

Joint of cold roast beef
joint cold boiled beef
2 ribs lamb
2 shoulders lamb
4 roast fowl
2 roast ducks
1 ham
1 tongue
2 veal & ham pies
2 pigeon pies
6 medium lobsters
1 collared calves head
18 lettuces
6 baskets of salad
6 cucumbers.

Stewed fruit
3doz pastry biscuits
2oz fruit turnovers
4doz cheesecakes
2 cold cabinet pud
22 blancmanges
a few jam puffs
1 plum pudding
cheese
6lbs butter
3doz rolls
2 plum cakes
$^1/_2$ lb tea.
Coffee not suitable for picnic
being difficult to make.

Making coffee seems a minor problem after preparing everything else. Our packet of crisps and a low fat yogurt type of picnic seems exceedingly inadequate and dull by comparison!

The big houses are now hotels and guesthouses, but tucked away above the harbour is another world, the real Seahouses, of rough stone dwellings where the fisherman lived, raising their families, mending their nets and lobster pots.

At the "Fisherman's Kitchen" at 2, South Street, you can feel exactly what life was like here one hundred years ago. This excellent business run by the Swallow family operates the last smokehouse in the village, curing herring and salmon. Their shop, which sells the best and widest range of fish for miles, is full of old photos, coopering tools and fishing tackle, bringing old Seahouses very much alive.

John Swallow moved here fifteen years ago after fishing with his own boat from North Shields. Now his son Andrew organises the day to day running of the smokehouse, which is open to visitors by prior appointment.

Local crab, lobster and salmon are sold here, also cod and haddock and the excellent Lindisfarne Oysters from John Sutherland at Ross Farm. Their kippers and smoked salmon are also special, delicately flavoured by the oak chippings in the smokehouse.

The original stables, where the herring girls used to sleep, are now store-rooms. In the shop Kathy and Julie can answer any questions you might have about fish and how to cook it. They are always experimenting to produce new treats to sell. Their pates, of kipper, mackerel, fresh and smoked salmon, are excellent and the smoked salmon, haddock and cod fish cakes are 90% fish. They have a heap of recipes, all printed out for their customers and a lethal looking weapon with which they will deftly open an oyster for you to try.

Salmon Soup

4 salmon heads, backbones and tails	*6 tomatoes, skinned, chopped*
	Juice and rind
2 tbspn olive oil	*2 oranges*
2 large onions, finely chopped	*4 bay leaves*

Steam salmon pieces for 4 minutes. Remove flesh and set aside. Place heads and bones in pan with 3pts water, cover and simmer for 1 1/2 hours. Sautee onion, tomatoes, oranges and bay leaves in olive oil until opaque. Strain fish stock into this, add fish, season, reheat gently and serve.

Much of the Swallow's fish ends up in the kitchen of The Olde Ship Hotel, run by Mr and Mrs Glen. Originally built as a farmhouse in 1745, it became an Inn, the oldest in the village, in 1812. It is a treasure chest of nautical bygones, figureheads, wheels, lamps and navigational instruments.

Jean Glen presides over the cooking, changing the menu daily and using a variety of local ingredients and some real Northumbrian recipes. Crab mayonnaise, fresh salmon, baked herring and Fisherman's Pie made with local cod and leeks are favourites. Traditional Beef stovies and Clootie Dumplings feature regularly on the menu and it is a pleasure to see them there.

It is a great pity that so few hotels offer regional specialities which are always appreciated by local customers and visitors, being simple, filling and delicious.

Mrs Glen's Beef Stovies

4 large sliced potatoes   2 tspns dripping from beef
4-6ozs cold roast beef   salt and pepper
2 medium onion

Melt dripping in heavy based stew pan, Add sliced onion, meat cut into pieces and potatoes in layers with seasoning. Cover pan with lid and cook slowly until potatoes are soft and floury.

Clootie Dumplings

$1^1/_4$ mixed dried fruit   1 tspn ginger
2 ozs mixed peel   1 tspn cinnamon
2 ozs halved glace cherries $^1/_2$ lb shredded suet
1 cup sugar   1 lb self raising flour
1 tspn mixed spice   milk to mix

Mix all dry ingredients and fruit. Mix well and gradually add milk until a soft dropping consistency is obtained. Put mixture into a scalded, floured cloth, tie with string allowing room for expansion. Place on a plate in a saucepan and fill with water to cover the plate. Simmer for 3 hours making sure it does not boil dry.

Near the harbour the Marine Life centre and Fishing museum is an imaginative mix of live fish and old memories, a sort of fishy "Yorvic" with smells of kippers and sounds of seagulls to assail the senses.

124

One of the most exciting things one can do in Seahouses is to leave it. Down the steep hill, past the Lifeboat, into the harbour and away on one of the brilliant boat trips to the Farne Islands.

Several local families, often ex fisherman, organise these tours which range from a 11/2 hour quick flick round the islands to a 5 hour marathon, landing on the Inner Farne and Staple Island and allowing plenty of time for bird and seal watching.

On a bright, sunny day, with the castle studded coast behind and the grey green puffin-filled sea all around it is a memorable journey.

The Farnes are a group of islands, many of them no more than huge rocks, visible only at low tide. The Inner Farne is the largest and was the retreat of Saint Aidan in 640 and St Cuthbert, the prior of Lindisfarne, came here in his old age in 676. At this time there was no fresh water and all the crops were eaten by the birds. Cuthbert prayed for help and was rewarded with a crystal spring and a heavy harvest.

The island's wild solitude continued to draw monks and hermits and in 1255 two Benedictines and their servants set up the House of Farne, which flourished with gifts of money and goods. They also developed local resources, keeping cattle, poultry and growing crops. They caught fish and seals and collected eggs. Selling seals was a profitable venture and in 1371, the monks of the day recorded that they had raised 27s 4d for "6 celys" which pleased them greatly as they were saving up to buy a special clock, a horalgium, which cost 45 shillings.

Two tiny chapels were built about this time dedicated to St Cuthbert and St Mary. St Cuthbert's with an original fourteenth century window still survives. The National Trust, who own the islands, charge a landing fee, so be prepared or you will have to remain on the boat and miss the chance to see your friends being attacked by the "comic terns" which dive bomb visitors with great accuracy, especially during the breeding season.

In the eighteenth century the Farnes were a favourite place for local gentry to indulge in mammoth picnics. A picture survives showing elegantly clad ladies with feathered hats and acres of hair and bewigged gentleman being served afternoon tea by a fleet of servants, who, in the next picture were banished to a rock to share a bun while their master's and mistresses sketched and strolled round the island.

In Victorian times, collecting eggs was a lucrative business. The egg gatherers risked life and limb, passing from pinnacle to pinnacle over a narrow board which made a bridge over the "horrid gaps".

Gulls and guillemots eggs were sent to London and were popular for making puddings. Gulls eggs were boiled and eaten cold as a luxury for breakfast. William Howitt wrote in 1841 that one such egg contained as much as three hen's eggs and was "tolerably good" but with a strong taste "which common people call a tang".

Between Seahouses and Bamburgh, nestling in the sand dunes, is Monk's House, looking out to the Farnes. Here the monks from the islands stored their goods. It was originally called Brock's Mouth and was given to the monks in 1257 by Henry III. Later owners were allowed to gather Eider duck eggs between May and July for the London market. The light down from the nests was used to fill coverings to lay on the beds, hence the eiderdown, much more romantic than a duvet.

In the nineteeth century a part of the steading was turned into a tavern, appropriately called St Cuthbert's Inn. Eider ducks are locally known as "Cuddy's chickens" as they were his close companions during his solitary retreats.

Whichever way you enter the village, it is dominated by the vast pink castle, $3/4$ of a mile long and 150 feet above the shore, it stands splendidly on the great Whinsill.

The site was fortified by the Ancient Britons. The Dinguardi tribes called it their "Citadel of Games" and it is also rumoured to be the "Joyous Garde" of Arthurian legend. In 547 it was rebuilt in magnificent red sandstone by King Ida, (no relation to the ducks) and in more recent times was owned by lord Crewe and finally Lord Armstrong of Cragside.Within the castle walls were vast granaries to feed the inhabitants when it was not safe to go shopping, which was quite often. A mill operated on the cliff to the North of the castle, grinding barley, oats and peas for the local poor.

Bamburgh 1910

There is a tale that around 1544 the people of Bamburgh suffered great hunger because the local fishermen could find no fish for over two years. The sea boiled and crashed and in the Spring "one terible beast" was washed onto the shore. The size of a man, it had "horns on the head o' it, red e'en, misshapen face, lucken(webbed) hands, feet and ane great rumple(?) hanging to the eird". Small wonder it frightened the fish!

The village is prettily placed around a green. The Lord Crewe Arms is the oldest and most interesting Inn. On the same terrace is Carter's first class butcher's shop. The business was founded in 1887 and over a hundred years later is still offering the same, locally reared, well butchered, properly hung meat, tender and well flavoured.

Mr Carter Jnr produces his own white pudding, haggis and pressed tongues, cooked on the premises to his grandfather's recipes. The special sausages, pork and chives, lamb and mint, pork and apple and a unique Bamburgh variety are of his own making. Mr Carter Senior makes superb pastry for the meat pies and his daughter in law produces fresh Scotch broth and Pea and Ham soup, for sale in handy containers. Local game, pheasant and wild duck is also available in season.

Eating well must be a Bamburgh tradition. In 1602 the Warden of the Middle Marches, Sir John Forster died leaving £1,020, a great fortune. In grand style he designated £544 to be spent on a stylish send off after his funeral. A contemporary account shows some of what was consumed.

13 gallons sack, 3 hogsheads wine, 7 stones butter, birds from Farnes, hops, 10 turkeys 21 pigs 12 dozen chickens.

The Church of St Aidan at the North end of the village was built in the 13th Century on the site where St Aidan died. Inside one can feel the centuries of prayers offered to protect the fishermen plying their trade in the cold and stormy north sea.

Just how stormy is known through the life and death of Grace Darling whose wonderful, Victorian Gothic memorial and grave are in the churchyard, looking back to the Longstone Lighthouse. From there Grace and her father set out on their epic adventure to rescue the survivors of the wrecked Forfarshire in September 1838. Just how incredible that rescue was brought home in the Grace Darling museum, just opposite the church. Here, in pride of place is the coble that Grace struggled to row. It is a big boat for two people to manage in a calm sea, but at night, in crashing seas beset by rocks it was indeed a miracle.

Following the coast North the road passes the mudflats of Budle Bay, well known for its variety of wading birds, geese, ducks and swans. Cockles used to be gathered here from September to March. For the lazy it was possible to hire a fisherman for 6p to carry you across the sands.

In the channel between Budle Point and Holy Island there used to be a famous oyster bed owned by the Earl of Tankerville. A severe frost and a low tide destroyed them all one winter and a new stock had to be brought from the Forth. A new bed has been successfully seeded by John Sutherland at nearby Ross an these Lindisfarne oysters cannot be bettered.

128

Grilled Creamed Oysters

Put a spoonful of cream over each oyster in its half shell, with a sprinkling of parmesan cheese and freshly ground black pepper. Cook under a pre heated grill for 3 minutes. Serve with bread and butter.

Fried Oysters

Remove oysters from shell. Dip in egg seasoned flour and fresh wholemeal breadcrumbs. Fry till golden in oil and butter. Serve with lemon wedges and Hollandaise or Tartar sauce.

We now follow the A1 until the turn off for Beal and Holy Island. It is vital to check the crossing times before setting off or you may spend a nerve wracking time dodging the waves or sitting on a platform provided for those who don't take these precautions.

Beal or Behill as it would have been called, is where the monks kept large apiaries to obtain honey for their mead. It might also have been the home of an Irish virgin Princess, St Bees or Begogh, who was a protege of St Aidan before becoming Abbess in her own convent. The hamlet has some ancient stone buildings and the farmhouse was once the mansion of the Selby family, dating back to 1674.

The history of food on Lindisfarne goes back to 8,000 B.C when evidence suggests Stone age came here, drawn perhaps by the wealth of easily gathered shellfish, fish and eggs.

Its fame as a holy place began in the seventh century when King Oswald, one of Northumbria's first Christian kings, welcomed Aidan, the young monk from Iona and offered him any site in his kingdom to form a ministry.

Aidan chose Lindisfarne as the perfect place for quiet contemplation. The first simple monastery included a refectory, kitchen and a kiln for baking bread. St Aidan encouraged the monks to fast. All during Lent, every Wednesday and Friday and in September and Advent.

St Aidans fasts were long and rigourous, but rules were made to be bent and tail of beaver, frogs, puffins and Barnacle geese were sometimes classed as fish and could be eaten on non-flesh days. The staple diet for the monks was grain pottages, bread, fish, a limited variety of vegetables and wild plants and sea birds which were often baked in clay.

Cuthbert, the shepherd lad, who when Prior of Melrose, made his first trip to the island was said to have been kept alive by a sea eagle who fed him fish and three pieces of dolphin which he found when he and his crew were driven ashore during a Winter storm. Soon after Cuthbert made his home on Lindisfarne. The monastery, bleak as it was, was not austere enough and he often retreated to a tiny island now called Cuddy's Isle to fast and pray.

From these days of denial, the monastery gradually became richer, surviving Viking assault. By the fifteenth century it was a busy community, the monks involved in farming, fishing, quarrying, brewing, baking and trading in iron, kelp and cloth.

The Scottish raiders were always a problem for food supplies, as much of the monks provisions came from the mainland. An old rhyme referring to the monk's records;

From Goswick we've geese, from Cheswick we've cheese
From Buckton we've venison in store,
From Swinhoe we've bacon, but the Scots have it taken
And the Prior is longing for more

A inventory of this period details 7 tons of salt, 7800 red herrings, 198 codlings, 2lbs Cyprus sugar, 2 boxes of ginger, 4lbs of saffron, 8lbs of pepper, 60lbs of almonds, 16lbs of rice, 7 flagons of olive oil, a basket of figs, beer and a whole sloopful of oysters. If this was an annual account they were either incredibly self indulgent or threw an awful lot of parties! They were fast becoming the sort of monks who needed to be "dissolved" in Henry VIII's reign.

A major source of food and income on the island in medieval times was the rabbit. This was not the result of a casual stroll with a ferret but an intensively managed, enclosed warren on the piece of land now known as The Snooks.

When myzomatosis nearly wiped out the rabbit population in the 1950's it was bad news for the Shelducks as the island foxes, realising rabbit was "off", substituted duck as their favourite dinner.

A lovely tale exists where, in the 1800's Islander's used Edible crabs instead of ferrets to frighten rabbits out of their burrows. According to Dr. George Johnson 1854, the male crab was sent down the hole with an inch long lighted candle on his back, thus alarming the rabbit who flew out into the waiting net. How one persuades a crab, especially one who can only breathe underwater and is therefore very dozy, to go down a hole and to expect the candle to stay alight is another story.

The ducks and geese which have always flocked here during migration provide welcome food for the Islanders. Lindisfarne is now a National Nature Reserve with wigeon, mallard, teal, pintail, Goldeneye and Barnacle, greylag and pinkfooted geese. Licen sed wildfowling is permitted. In Victorian times the deadly punt could kill up to a hundred birds at a time.

There is still an annual "Duck Supper" on the Island. This used to take place at the Iron Rails tavern but is now hosted by the Masseys at the Lindisfarne Hotel. At the end of the shooting season each gun takes his own goose to be cooked, and this, with the broth and vegetables generously donated by the patrons turn the evening into a feast.

Tourism came to the island in the 1700's and has flourished ever since. At one time there were ten inns, The Ship, Brittania, Iron Rails, Selby Arms, Crow and Anchor, Cambridge House, Northumberland Arms and the Castle Hotel. The fare was decidedly fishy and the whole population was involved in catching lobster, crab, cod and herring. The original three storey herring house, now converted still stands on the way to the castle as does the old smoke house behind what used to be the Iron Rails Inn.

Skate was a common fish here and it was laid on the roofs of the houses to dry before being enjoyed by the fishermen, washed down with a pint of beer.

Skate with Butter

12 ozs skinned skate wings, cut
into 2
2 ozs herb butter
1 tbspn parsley

2 tbspns lemon juice
seasoning

Place wings in a shallow pan and add approx 1/2pt of boiling water. Poach for about ten minutes. Remove and keep warm on a serving dish. Melt butter in a pan, add parsley, lemon juice and seasonong. Cook until golden brown. Pour over fish and serve.

The Priory, Holy Island. 1900

At the Manor Hotel, next to the priory, Jennifer and George Ward have been using the harvest from the sea for the past ten years. No nonsense, wholesome food is served here. Crab, lobster and salmon are cooked simply and served with fresh vegetables, broccoli, beans, potatoes and herbs from the hotel garden. Wigeon casseroled in stout is another local dish.

Lunches are difficult to cater for as the tides can prevent visitors from arriving until late in the day. In the evening the menu often includes local white fish or

Pan Hacklety; real Northumbrian fare or a wonderful hotch potch created by Jennifer's mother and known to the family as "Grandma Beattie's Few Soup". Calling a broth "them" is a specifically Northumbrian trait. This particular concoction is a glorious mix of real stock made the day before, carrots, leeks, lentils, barley, forcemeat, onion and any interesting game, rabbit or pheasant. A meal in itself.

To get the full flavour of the island it is best to walk. The Museum of Island life, run by Ingrid Ward, which vivdly recaptures Lindisfarnes' past, is a good place to start. The village is compact, the stone cottages low to escape the winds. The ruined proiry, protected by a striking statue of St Aidan, hand raised in benediction, still feels a very holy place. It was built in 1093 after the style of Whitby Abbey and designed to attract pilgrims, the tourists of the day.

To feed these visitors and make money the monks employed laymen to fish and farm, grow hemp and flax, beans, onion and leeks and hay for the animals. They also rented out "holiday cottages" and were not above pilfering when a ship was wrecked.

The thirteenth century church of St Mary's is the site of a pagan custom where newly married couples have a cake broken over their heads to ensure future health, wealth and fertility. If it were only that simple.

Lindisfarne Castle

The twentieth century castle designed by Lutyens, standing impregnable on Beblowe Crag was at first no other than a tiny Tudor fort. Because it had a good harbour it was seen as a useful place from which to launch attacks on the Scottish coast. The island, though "all sett with fishers poore" had good enough store houses, brew and bakehouses to "conserve and prepare victualls sufficient to furnish the said navye" and the priory church became the garrison's main store.

By 1901 the "daintie little fort" was disintegrating. Edward Hudson, the founder of "Country Life" fell in love with it and commissioned Edward Lutyens to convert it. This he did most successfully turning the ruin into a cosy and romantic home with breathtaking views from every window.

The kitchen, with its stone flagged floor, huge range, high backed oak settle and refectory table also houses the means to operate the portcullis over the entrance.

Hudson however, was a most hospitable man who entertained politicians, musicians and Royalty to frequent lavish house parties. Edwardian food was famously elegant and many recipes from great Northumbrian houses are recorded.

A possible menu might have included;

Lindisfarne Rich Lobster Soup, Salmon Trout in cream, Cheviot Lamb Cutlets and Wild Bramble Cream

Lindisfarne Rich Lobster Soup

Remove lobster from shell. Keep claws. Wash shell and pound it with butter.

1 small lobster

2 ozs butter 1

bay leaf

1 sprig parsley

seasoning

2 tspns lemon juice

1 $^1/_2$ pts good fish stock

1 $^1/_2$ ozs cornflour

$^1/_2$ pt cream

Put in saucepan with bay leaf, seasoning, parsley, lemon juice and cornflour. Cook gently, stirring well until nicely coloured, approx ten minutes. Add stock and rough;ly chopped flesh and coral and simmer for forty minutes. Pass through a fine sieve to remove gritty shell. Stir in cream and add diced claw meat. Reheat but do not boil and serve.

Wild Bramble Cream

1 lb blackberries
3 apples
rind of 1 lemon
$^1/_4$ lb sugar
$^3/_4$ pt cream

$^3/_4$ oz gelatine
3 drops carmine (red colour-
ing)
2 tbspns water

Put blackberries in pan with lemon rind, sugar and apple, peeled and thinly sliced. Stew gently until soft stirring frequently. Rub mixture through a hair sieve. Dissolve gelatine in two tbspns water and strain into puree. Fold in cream, whipped and add colouring. Pour into a wet mould and leave to set.

Back on the mainland, we turn left onto the A1 and Belford. Audrey Atkins Belford Craft Gallery is the hub of the village, where posters are put up and local chat swapped amidst the range of pottery and paintings and craftwork by Northumbrian artists. The shop is extremely well stocked with tourist information and Audrey has compiled her own comprehensive list of places to eat in the area with copies of menus and tariffs.

At the back of the Gallery is the Singin Hinny Tea Room initiated by Audrey and now run by Lisa Smith. Here the Hinnys, a local term of endearment, are made on a griddle and sing as they are cooked, for all to hear, and are then enjoyed, fresh and warm with tea or coffee.

Belford Singin' Hinnies

250gms plain flour
125grms best butter
1 level tspn baking powder

pinch of salt
Handful of currants
$^1/_4$pt of sour milk

Mix flour, baking powder and salt and rub in the butter, but not too finely. Throw in the currants and mix with the milk to a wettish scone consistency. Divide into six and roll into balls, using well floured hands. Roll out thinly and cook on a girdle or heavy frying pan until golden and speckly. When the little lumps of butter sizzle you will hear them singing.

Belford, now bypassed, was once on the main London to Edinburgh coach route and the Blue Bell Hotel a busy post house. In Charles I time it was described as the "most miserable, beggarly town of sods that was ever made in an afternoon of loam and stocks. (The sods being a reference to building materials, rather than the inhabitants?) "In all the town not a loaf of bread, nor a quart of beer or a lock of hay or a peck of oats and little shelter for horse or man" was available.

Rejoining the A1 and heading for Alnwick we make a brief detour to Ellingham, a haven of history amidst the rich arable lands of the coastal plain. Ellingham Hall, built in the seventeeth century was the home of the Haggerston family. The West wing adjoins a small Roman catholic chapel built in 1600. In 1750 a priest, trying to avoid a religious persecution wrote a disguised account of his activities "salary from factory, £30 and a field valued at £8. No helps unless a little beef from the Haggerstons. About one hundred and five customers to my shop".

136

Of particular interest to the gourmet is the Ellingham Wild Boar Company, the venture of Caroline and Graham Simpson. Run from Ellingham Home Farm, Graham, like many farmers looked for ways to diversify on his 650 acres and with great flair decided to try wild boar.

As natives to Northumberland, boar used to roam freely in the extensive ancient woodlands until the late seventeenth century. Fierce and independant they were never domesticated, but provided sport for the nobility.

Graham now has a breeding herd of twenty sows and a massive 400lb boar of Polish/German extraction. The sows can farrow until they are twelve to fourteen years old. This is no doubt because they have so little stress at Ellingham, compared to the appalling lives of intensively farmed sows who are used like machines to pump out piglets.

Here the sows roam and rootle and make nests for their offspring, producing them effortlessly. The boarlets, usually born in the spring, rampage at will, in the charge of a 'nanny' sow and suckling from any handy mother. They wean themselves at three to four months and all Graham has to do is provide food, shelter and leave them to it. His feed, turnips and Jordan's pig nuts, is such that the meat is 99% organic. They are wormed once a year and are so healthy and hardy that they never need anything else.

Graham likens the meat to a cross between venison and beef, fine textured and lean, with a flavour never found in insipid factory farmed food. Because of their wedge shape and constant exercise, the fore end joints are as good, if not better, than the rump. The males are kept until they are twelve to sixteen months and weigh about 120lbs. The meat is jointed by a local butcher and returned to the farm from where it is packed and sold. Sausages are also made and these and the meat are becoming very popular with hotels, The Warenford Lodge, among others, is supplied by Graham.

Caroline Simpson, a Cordon Bleu cook and an expert on cooking this versatile meat has provided several tried and tested recipes. The marinades include strong complimentary flavours, juniper is especially good.

Wild Boar Cutlets

2 lbs wild boar cutlets
3 juniper berries
buttermilk flour
seasoning

Leave the cutlets lying in the buttermilk for three days. Dry with a cloth, rub with salt and pounded juniper berries. Roast or grill the cutlets. If roasting, put in a pan with a little boiling water and baste from time to time with the buttermilk. When the meat is tender, thicken the sauce with flour and serve cutlets in their own sauce.

Fricassee of Young Wild Boar

4 lbs wild boar, cut into bite size chunks
2 fl oz calvados
15fl oz red wine
5 fl oz double cream

Marinade

3^1/$_2$ ozs sliced onions   *ground black pepper*
1 sliced carrot   *2 pt red wine*
2 halved garlic cloves   *2 fl oz calvados*
1 bouquet garni   *2 fl oz cider vinegar*
pinch of cayenne   *3^1/$_2$ fl oz nut oil*
tspn sea salt

Put meat in a large bowl and marinade, add oil last. Leave at room temp. for 48 hours, turning occasionally. Remove meat, saute in butter in large, heavy bottomed casserole. When the meat has browned, de-glaze with the calvados and flame. Add wine and equal amount of strained marinade to cover meat. Puree all herbs and vegetables from the marinade and add to dish. Cover and simmer for 1 hour, add more wine if needed. Remove meat to a warmed dish. Add cream to the sauce stir over a low heat and pour over meat just before serving.

We now return to Alnwick. It is well worth turning to the right onto the old A1 to enter Alnwick over the Lion Bridge for the best view of the castle. Film companies from all over the world have used this approach for their scenes of medieval mayhem. A certain local extra, a Gloucester Old Spot pig named Boadicea, is remembered for her Miss Piggy-like histrionics which resulted in her uprooting half of the perfect turf in the castle courtyard before retiring to her Craster home to produce generations of superb pork.

We have come all the way back to Alnwick to finish our tour at John Blackmores, a small restaurant with one of the very best reputations in the North. Booking in advance is essential but very worthwhile.

Situated in Narrowgate, leading from the castle into the town, John has turned one of the historic hourses in Dorothy Foster court into a centre for serious food lovers. All the ingredients are local and fresh and the recipes are created by John who was head chef at a leading country house hotel.

There are only a few tables so that the service is excellent and the food freshly cooked for each person. There is no pressure to hurry, in fact the opposite as endless cups of coffee and fresh cream chocolates are offered at the end of the meal. John and his wife Penny are the people who create new traditions of Northumbrian food. If only there were more like them.

RECIPE INDEX

Meat and Vegetables

GAME

Poultry

Fish and Shellfish

Puddings

Hasty Pudding	33
Mrs Armstrong's Favourite Lemon Pudding	95
Mrs Glasses Whipped Syllabub	60
North Country Savoury Pudding	45
Wild Bramble Cream	135

Baking

Barley Bread	35
Belford Signin Hinnies	136
Berwick May Day Tarts	6
Duke of Northumberland Cake	109
Farm Pound Cake	42
Harvest Cake	46
Honey Cakes	14
Mrs Dunn's Soft Gingerbread	49
Northumbrian Farmhouse Fruit Cake	31
Nun's Biskett	35
Oatmeal Cakes	16
Overnight Spice Loaf	46
Seed Cake	90
Victorian Simple Sponge	60
Whittingham Buttons	48

Miscellaneous

Blackberry and Sloe Jelly	68
Bee Wine	14
Broom Wine	102
Rosemary or Lavender Sugar	78

Maureen Emmerson, Jill's Aunt, has lived in Canada for over thirty years. These wonderful graphics, inspired by her love of Northumberland, were drawn during one of her regular visits to her family near Rothbury. Many of them had to be finished when she returned home, but luckily have survived their transatlantic crossing back to England.